EASY PIZZA RECIPE BOOK

100+ Authentic Italian Pizza Recipes. A Complete Cookbook: to Learn Special Pizza and Focaccia Dough for Homemade Pizza from scratch! Many Gourmets Toppings Suggestion for Every Taste!

By

ANTHONY CRACCOLO

TABLE OF CONTENT

INTRODUCTION

In this book, you will find a wide variety of pizza dough recipes; they result from experiments or old recipes adapted to my way of making pizza. The purpose of this book is to share easy recipes. Some are classic while others are out of the ordinary, but the most important thing is that there is a recipe for everyone. Keep in mind that we are not in a chemistry lab, so when we talk about pizza dough, we cannot use recipes that give authentic ingredients.

For example, each type of flour (even if it is classified as the same type but produced by a different mill) can vary significantly. Therefore, we must be willing to adapt.

This is especially true with the choice of flour, but it is also true with other ingredients.

So here's my advice: always be wary of recipes that give you with absolute certainty the working times for the leavening processor that do not take into account the flour, room temperature, etc., to be used. These characteristics may seem irrelevant at first, but in reality, they greatly influence the final result. So instead, learn to develop an eye and a feel for the characteristics of the dough, learn about the rising process, and indulge in the experiences that the dough has to offer.

Flour

When mastering a specific type of dough, it is essential to know all the used ingredients.

I recommend experimenting with different types of flour and then choosing the one you like best, the one that suits your purposes, which you can then replicate over and over again without any problems.

Each type of flour, especially those of different strengths, has an additional capacity for absorbing water.

Capacity. Therefore, the amount of water required in recipes may need a slight adjustment.

The "W" index indicates the strength of a specific dough and its resistance to rising.

This is valuable information when preparing bread.

However, as you may have already noticed, no markings indicate the strength of the flour you buy at the supermarket. The problem can be solved by consulting the percentage of protein in the flour, as this indicates the strength of the flour.

Furthermore, various types of flour are available on the market, and they vary according to the degree of refining and the kind of wheat used to produce them. This book will only focus on flours suitable for breadmaking (and therefore ideal for pizza dough).

The most suitable flours are simple, strong, very strong, and wholemeal.

Plain flour is one of the most common types of flour and is the most refined of the four discussed options. For this reason, it has the lowest strength (the lowest W index) compared to the other flours. During the refining process, it has been deprived of a particular element,s including protein, which means it also contains less gluten, which is essential for forming the gluten mesh. Regular flour has a protein content of 9% to 11.5%. This type of flour is called 'all-purpose flour' in the USA.

Strong flour has a protein content of around 14% to 16%. This makes it the perfect flour for baking bread and pizza. It will cause the dough to develop a more excellent gluten mesh during kneading, which will support the rising process and allow for more excellent water absorption. This type of flour is known in the USA as bread flour. On the other hand, solid flour has a fine texture and can be used in baked goods that require a long rising time. In this case, the protein content is more than 13% and creates a very elastic dough with a very dense and complex gluten network. Therefore, if you live in the US, look for bread flour with the highest protein content.

Finally, whole wheat flour is the flour that has undergone minor refining processes and therefore has more fiber than other types of flour. As a result, its protein content is typically higher than 14%. However, it should be noted that the high protein percentage is not always directly proportional to the gluten that will develop during kneading.

For this reason, I always recommend mixing this flour with other types to create a more substantial dough with a good mesh of gluten. This type of flour is known in the United States as whole wheat flour.

These are the guidelines for the most popular types of pizza flour found in supermarkets. Of course, it would be a different story if you decided to shop at the mall, where they now enjoy experimenting with new processes and combinations of flours that create excellent results. However, if you insist on buying flour at the supermarket, I urge you to read the protein content on the label to find out the approximate strength of the flour. The more information you can retrieve, the more confident you will be in their final performance.

The malt

In the following recipes, you will often find the addition of malt. This ingredient, which is particularly suitable for professional bakery products, is beneficial for improving the dough's rise and enhancing the aroma and color. If you cannot find this ingredient, you can replace it with the same amount of acacia honey or simple caster sugar.

1) CLASSIC THIN CRUST PIZZA DOUGH

Preparation Time: 2 hours   **Cooking Time:** 0 minutes   **Servings: 4**

Ingredients:

- ✓ 2 tbsp s dry active yeast
- ✓ 1 cup lukewarm water
- ✓ 4 cups flour

Directions:

- ❖ In a large bowl, dissolve the yeast in the water. Combine the flour, oil, and salt. Then stir the flour into the yeast mixture in small batches. The dough should start to become smooth and pull away from the sides of the bowl. If it doesn't, adjust water and flour amounts as necessary.
- ❖ Cover your work surface with a dusting of flour and quickly knead the dough until it becomes elastic and easy to work with.

Ingredients:

- ✓ 2 tbsp s extra virgin olive oil
- ✓ 1 ½ tsp salt

- ❖ Oil a clean bowl and place the dough in it; cover with lightly oiled plastic wrap. Allow the dough to rise in a warm spot for 1 to 3 hours or until it has doubled in size.

2) PIZZA DOUGH WITH RYE FLOUR

Preparation Time: 2 hours   **Cooking Time:** 0 minutes   **Servings: 4**

Ingredients:

- ✓ Biga:
- ✓ 130 g of Strong Flour
- ✓ 3 g of fresh yeast
- ✓ 70 mL of water
- ✓ Dough:

Directions:

- ❖ Prepare the biga: dissolve 3 g of fresh yeast in 70 mL of water and mix with 130 g of strong flour;
- ❖ Once the dough is homogeneous, let it rest at room temperature for about 8 hours;
- ❖ Prepare the dough: dissolve the biga in 220 mL of water, add 100 g of rye flour, 175 g of strong flour and 1 heaped tsp of salt;
- ❖ Knead until you get a smooth and homogeneous dough;
- ❖ Let it rise for 3 hours and then spread it out on an oiled baking sheet;
- ❖ Let it leaven for another 2 hours repaired by drafts;
- ❖ Proceed with topping and cooking the pizza.

Ingredients:

- ✓ Biga
- ✓ 100 g of Rye Flour
- ✓ 180 g of Strong Flour
- ✓ 1 heaped tsp of salt (about 7 g)
- ✓ 220 mL of water
- ❖ Recommended topping!
- ❖ I would eat this rye dough pizza with the following toppings:
- ❖ Pumpkin sauce (see chapter 9)
- ❖ around 16 anchovies in olive oil
- ❖ 150 g of buffalo mozzarella
- ❖ Directions:
- ❖ Once the dough has leavened in the tray, define the edge with a spoon, which you will leave without topping (and will form the crust), then pour the pumpkin sauce previously seasoned with oil and salt and put the pizza to bake; About halfway through cooking (after 10 minutes), take if out and top the pizza with mozzarella and let it bake until cooked;
- ❖ Finally, add the anchovies.

3) THE SANDWICH DOUGH

Preparation Time: 2 hours   **Cooking Time:** 4 minutes   **Servings: 0**

Ingredients:
- ✓ 330 g of Wholemeal Strong Flour
- ✓ 240 mL of water
- ✓ 3 g of dry yeast

Directions:

❖ Thanks to this recipe, we are going to prepare a super club sandwich!

❖ Dissolve 3 g of yeast in 240 mL of water and start kneading by adding 330 g of flour little by little;

❖ After a few minutes, add 1 generous tsp of salt, 3 tbsp s of oil and put the dough into the dough point;

❖ When the dough is smooth and homogeneous, place it in the fridge in an airtight oiled container for 12h;

❖ Take the dough out from the fridge and divide it into 3 equal parts, form 3 balls and let them acclimate for 3 hours at about 25°C/77°F;

❖ Once the dough has been relaxed, helping yourself with a rolling pin, stretch out the three balls until you obtain a disc with a classic thickness for pizza, place them in layers one on top of the other, greasing them with oil; Bake the pizza.

Ingredients:
- ✓ 3 tbsp s of EVO oil (about 21 g)
- ✓ 1 heaped tsp of salt (about 7 g)

❖ Recommended topping!

❖ Ingredients for 3 people:

❖ 3 fried eggs

❖ 9 slices of bacon

❖ 1 big beef tomatoes

❖ lettuce

❖ Mary Rose sauce (mix of mayonnaise and ketchup in a 4:1 ratio)

❖ EVO oil

❖ salt

❖ chives

❖ Method:

❖ Pan-fry the chives with a drizzle of oil until taking color; Open the eggs directly in the pan over the chives and fry them (over-easy), in the meantime cook the bacon separately; Once the 3 doughs have been taken out of the oven, place the eggs (season them with oil and salt) with the sliced tomatoes on the first layer, in the second layer, add the bacon, lettuce and a drop of oil; Add the Mary Rose sauce and finalize the club sandwich with the last layer of dough; At this point, you just have to cut the sandwich into wedges of the desired size and serve.

❖ Tip: A simpler but excellent way is not to divide the dough into 3 discs but to create a single thicker disc to stretch and put it in the oven. Obviously, it will come very often compared to a classic pizza, but once it is cooked, I suggest you open it in half with a knife and stuff it with pecorino fondue and mortadella.

4) PIZZA DOUGH WITH SPELT FLOUR

Preparation Time: 2 hours　　　　**Cooking Time:** 0 minutes　　　　**Servings: 4**

Ingredients:

- ✓ 180 g of Strong Flour
- ✓ 90 g of Spelt Flour
- ✓ 90 g of Wholemeal Flour
- ✓ 250 mL of water
- ✓ 4 g of dry yeast

Ingredients:

- ✓ 2 tbsp s of extra
- ✓ virgin olive oil (14 g)
- ✓ 1 heaped tsp of
- ✓ salt (about 7 g)

Directions:

- ❖ Dissolve 4 g of dry yeast in 250 mL of water and start kneading by gradually adding the three types of flour;
- ❖ After a few minutes, add 2 tbsp s of oil and 1 heaped tsp of salt;
- ❖ Continue to knead until you get a smooth and compact dough;
- ❖ Let it rest for an hour, then place it in the fridge to mature in an airtight and oiled container for 24 hours;
- ❖ Remove the dough from the fridge, place it on an oiled baking tray and let it acclimatize for about 1 hour;
- ❖ Start stretching out the dough following the advice I left you in chapter 1;
- ❖ After around 3/4 hours, proceed with topping and cooking the pizza.
- ❖ Recommended topping!
- ❖ Also this time I would like to recommend an excellent stuffing with chicory and sausage.
- ❖ Here are the ingredients and the procedure to make it:
- ❖ 125 g of smoked cheese
- ❖ 125 g mozzarella

- ❖ Chicory
- ❖ 300 g of Italian sausage
- ❖ 1 clove of garlic
- ❖ 1 fresh chili pepper
- ❖ EVO oil
- ❖ Salt
- ❖ Sear the chicory in boiling salted water (it must be nice and soft), drain it, cut it and sauté it
- ❖ in a pan with oil, garlic and chili; Take out the sausage casing, cut it into small pieces, and cook them separately for about fifteen minutes. Begin to top the pizza with most of the previously cut smoked cheese and mozzarella, keeping 2 handfuls aside; Add chicory, sausage and a drizzle of EVO oil. Bake the pizza until about halfway through cooking time (around 10 minutes), add the remaining smoked cheese, and put it in the oven again to get a beautiful golden-brown color.

5) PIZZA DOUGH WITH OAT FLOUR

Preparation Time: 2 hours   **Cooking Time**: 0 minutes   **Servings: 4**

Ingredients:
- ✓ 370 g of Strong Flour
- ✓ 50 g of oat flour
- ✓ 260 mL of water

Ingredients:
- ✓ 3 g of fresh yeast
- ✓ 3 tbsp s of EVO oil (about 20 g)
- ✓ 1 large tsp salt (about 7 g)

Directions:

- ❖ Start by dissolving 3 g of fresh yeast in 260 mL of water;
- ❖ Add the flour and after mixing for a few minutes add 1 tsp of salt;
- ❖ Add 3 tbsp s of EVO oil and knead until you reach a smooth and homogeneous mass;
- ❖ Place the dough in an airtight container and let it mature in the fridge for 12 hours;
- ❖ Remove the dough from the fridge, place it on an oiled baking tray and let it acclimatize for about an hour;
- ❖ Proceed stretching the dough in the pan following the advice you find in chapter 1;
- ❖ Once stretched, let it rise for 3 or 4 hours;
- ❖ Once it has doubled in volume, proceed with topping and cooking the pizza.
- ❖ Recommended topping!
- ❖ A great way to fill this pizza is to use a perfect combination: eggs and asparagus.

- ❖ Ingredients:
- ❖ Asparagus sauce (see chapter 9)
- ❖ 2 eggs
- ❖ pecorino cheese (or Grana Padano)
- ❖ stracchino (or cream if you can't find it)
- ❖ asparagus
- ❖ EVO oil
- ❖ salt, lime
- ❖ Parma Ham
- ❖ Method:
- ❖ Boil the fresh asparagus for 60/90 seconds, and then cool them down using iced water;
- ❖ Cut the asparagus into rings and marinate them with extra virgin olive oil, salt, zest, and lime juice.
- ❖ Stretch the dough on the baking tin, and once is doubled in volume, pour the asparagus cream, the stracchino, the asparagus rings, and the eggs.
- ❖ Bake the pizza until is golden-brown.
- ❖ Take the pizza out of the oven, top it with pecorino cheese, Parma ham and a drop of EVO oil.

6) PIZZA DOUGH RECIPE WITH SPELT FLOUR

Preparation Time: 2 hours   **Cooking Time:** 0 minutes   **Servings: 4**

Ingredients:

- ✓ 120 g of mother yeast
- ✓ 200 g of Spelt Flour
- ✓ 40 gr of Strong Flour
- ✓ 120 mL of water

Directions:

- ❖ Dissolve 120 g of mother yeast in 120 mL of water and 1 tsp of malt;
- ❖ Start kneading by adding the flour (200 g of spelt flour and 40 g of strong flour) a little at a time,
- ❖ When the flour is incorporated, add 3 tbsp s of oil and 1 heaped tsp of salt;
- ❖ Knead until you get a smooth and homogeneous mixture;
- ❖ Do a round of folds every 20 minutes, for three times;
- ❖ Put the dough into an airtight container and let it rise for 3 hours;
- ❖ Stretch the dough on an oiled baking sheet and let it rise for 2 hours;
- ❖ When the dough has doubled in volume, proceed with topping and baking it.
- ❖ Recommended topping!
- ❖ A great match could be yellow cherry tomatoes, eggplant pesto and crispy bacon!

Ingredients:

- ✓ 3 tbsp s of EVO oil (21 g)
- ✓ 1 large tsp of salt (about 7 g)
- ✓ 1 tsp of malt (about 3 g)

- ❖ Ingredients:
- ❖ 250 g of eggplant pesto (see chapter 9)
- ❖ 100 g of yellow cherry tomatoes
- ❖ 125 g of mozzarella
- ❖ 100 g of bacon
- ❖ pecorino cheese
- ❖ Directions:
- ❖ Once the pizza dough is stretched out and leavened, pour some aubergine pesto on the dough; If you prefer, you can use a normal tomato sauce to go classic and add the aubergine pesto at the end of cooking;
- ❖ Bake it for about 10 minutes (until half cooked) then add the mozzarella and the half-cut cherry tomatoes; Once ready, add the previously pan-fried bacon and the pecorino cheese.

7) PIZZA DOUGH RECIPE WITH TURMERIC

Preparation Time: 2 hours   **Cooking Time:** 0 minutes   **Servings: 4**

Ingredients:

- ✓ 230 g of Strong Flour
- ✓ 60 g of Wholemeal Flour
- ✓ 120 g of mother yeast
- ✓ 190 mL of water

Ingredients:

- ✓ 1/2 tsp of malt (about 3 g)
- ✓ 1 tbsp of EVO oil (7 g)
- ✓ 1 large tsp of salt (about 7 g)
- ✓ 1/2 tsp of turmeric

Directions:

- ❖ Dissolve 120 g of mother yeast in 190 mL of water together with 1/2 tsp of malt;
- ❖ Add the two types of flour and start kneading;
- ❖ Add 1 generous tsp of salt and ½ tsp of turmeric;
- ❖ Finally add 1 tbsp of oil and knead until reaching the dough point;
- ❖ Let it rest for 20 minutes, then do a round of folds every 20 minutes, for 1 hour;
- ❖ Then, place the dough in an airtight container and let it rest in the fridge for 12 hours;
- ❖ Take the dough out of the fridge, place it in the center of an oiled pan and cover it with cling film; Let the dough acclimate for about 2 hours, then start stretching it following the advice I left you in chapter 1;
- ❖ Let it rise for about 3 hours until it has doubled in volume;
- ❖ Proceed with topping and cooking it!

- ❖ Recommended topping!
- ❖ How about topping this fantastic yellow dough with a mixture of cheeses and speck?
- ❖ Ingredients:
- ❖ 125 g of mozzarella
- ❖ 80 g of brie
- ❖ 60 g of gorgonzola
- ❖ 50 g of cream
- ❖ Parmesan Cheese
- ❖ 100 g of Speck
- ❖ Walnuts
- ❖ Directions:
- ❖ Top the pizza using the cream as a base, and place the cheeses on the top, until they cover the
- ❖ entire pizza (but mind to the crust!);
- ❖ Once baked, add speck, flaked parmesan and walnuts.

8) PIZZA DOUGH RECIPE WITH SEMOLINA FLOUR

Preparation Time: 2 hours   **Cooking Time**: 0   **Servings: 4**

Ingredients:
- ✓ 225 g of Very Strong Flour
- ✓ 50 grams of Wholemeal Flour
- ✓ 50 g of Semolina Flour
- ✓ 60 g of mother yeast
- ✓ 160 mL of water

Ingredients:
- ✓ 50 mL of sparkling white wine
- ✓ 1/2 tsp of malt (about 3gr)
- ✓ 3 tbsp s of EVO oil (21 g)
- ✓ 1 heaped tsp of salt (about 7 g)

Directions:
- ❖ Dissolve 60 g of mother yeast in 160 mL of water, 50 mL of sparkling wine and 1/2 tsp of malt;
- ❖ Start kneading by adding the three types of flour and lastly 1 heaped tsp of salt; Knead for a few minutes, then add 3 tbsp s of oil, bringing the dough to reach the "dough point";
- ❖ Let the dough rest for 20 minutes, then make three series of folds (one every 20 minutes);
- ❖ Place the dough in an oiled container and put it to rest in the fridge for 36 hours;
- ❖ Take it out of the fridge (at least 5 hours before cooking) and let it acclimatize for about half an hour; Place the dough in the center of the oiled pan and, after 2 hours, stretch it;
- ❖ After a couple of hours, once the dough has risen, proceed with topping and baking it.

- ❖ Recommended topping!
- ❖ This dough goes divinely with fresh figs and Parma ham, don't you think?
- ❖ Here are the ingredients for this sheet pan pizza:
- ❖ 125 g of Burrata (mozzarella if you can't find it)
- ❖ 4 fresh figs
- ❖ 6/8 slices of Parma ham (thinly sliced)
- ❖ 200g Burrata or buffalo mozzarella
- ❖ Method:
- ❖ Stretch and bake the pizza with a drizzle of EVO oil;
- ❖ Once turns golden-brown, take it out and add the figs, the Parma ham, and the burrata.

9) HOUR HERBED ARTISAN DOUGH

Preparation Time: 2 hours   **Cooking Time**: 0 minutes   **Servings: 4**

Ingredients:
- ✓ ½ tsp active dry yeast
- ✓ ¼ cup lukewarm water
- ✓ 3 cups flour
- ✓ 1 cup milk

Ingredients:
- ✓ 2 ½ tbsp s olive oil
- ✓ 1 tsp salt
- ✓ 2 tbsp s chopped basil
- ✓ 2 tbsp s chopped oregano

Directions:
- ❖ Place the yeast in lukewarm water until foamy. Then combine the yeast mixture and flour in a large mixing bowl by whisking together. Then add the milk and the oil. Use your hands to mix the ingredients until a loose dough forms; add the salt and herbs. Knead a couple of times no more until ball forms. If the dough is sticky, it's okay.

- ❖ Into an oiled bowl, let the dough ball and cover with oiled wax paper followed by a layer of plastic wrap. Let the bowl in a warm place for 24 hours. 3 to 4 hours before the 24-hour period is complete, carefully turn the dough ball in the bowl and recover to finish rising.

10) ITALIAN CHEESE DOUGH

Preparation Time: 2 hours   **Cooking Time:** 0 minutes   **Servings: 4**

Ingredients:

- ✓ 1 cup lukewarm water
- ✓ ¼ cup olive oil, plus additional
- ✓ 1 tsp honey

Ingredients:

- ✓ 2 ¼ tsp active dry yeast
- ✓ 3 cups flour, plus additional
- ✓ 1/2 cup freshly grated Parmigiano-Reggiano cheese

Directions:

- ❖ In a large bowl, combine the water, oil, and honey; sprinkle yeast on top. The mixture should have a foamy appearance after 5 to 8 minutes.

- ❖ In a separate bowl, mix together the flour and cheese. Slowly add the flour mixture to the yeast mixture, stirring as you go. The dough should be soft and a bit sticky so adjust water and flour amounts as necessary. Keep mixing until the dough begins to have an elastic appearance.

- ❖ Flour your work surface and begin to knead the dough just until it becomes smooth.

- ❖ Oil a large bowl and place your dough in it, turning it several times to make sure the dough gets oiled lightly on all sides. Place oiled plastic wrap over the bowl and set it in a warm location. Allow the dough to rise until it has more than doubled in size (about 1 to 3 hours).

- ❖ Before using the dough, knead on a floured work area for another minute so that it returns to a smooth and elastic state and so that any extra oil gets absorbed.

11) WHOLE WHEAT PIZZA DOUGH

Preparation Time: 2 hours   **Cooking Time:** 0 minutes   **Servings: 4**

Ingredients:

- ✓ 1 cup lukewarm water
- ✓ ¼ cup olive oil
- ✓ 1 tsp sugar
- ✓ 2 ¼ tsp active dry yeast

Ingredients:

- ✓ 2 ¼ cups flour
- ✓ ¾ cup whole wheat flour
- ✓ ¼ tsp salt

Directions:

- ❖ In a large bowl, combine the water, oil, and sugar; sprinkle yeast on top. The mixture should have a foamy appearance when it's ready, about 5 to 8 minutes.

- ❖ In a separate bowl, sift the flours together with the salt. Working slowly, begin to add the flour mixture to the yeast mixture, adding just a little at a time and stirring constantly. Adjust flour or water amounts appropriately so that your dough looks soft and just a bit sticky.

- ❖ Flour your work surface and quickly knead the dough until it becomes smooth – don't overwork it. Oil a clean bowl and put the dough in it, turning a few times so that all sides of the dough are covered lightly with oil. Cover the bowl with oiled plastic wrap and place in a warm spot. Let the dough rise until it has doubled in size (1 to 3 hours depending on how warm the spot is).

- ❖ Before using the dough, knead on a floured work area for another minute so that it returns to a smooth and elastic state and so that any extra oil gets absorbed.

- ❖ Advice

- ❖ Pizza dough made with whole-wheat flour takes twice as much time to rise.

- ❖ The whole meal flours absorb much water than refined flours. For that matter, the water amounts on the recipe are just indicative and it's upon you to feel the dough consistency obtained and add little water if it is too hard.

- ❖ To get an easier product to work on, most of the dough is made by adding a percentage of refined flour and a percentage of whole-wheat flour.

12) RUSTIC COUNTRYSIDE DOUGH

Preparation Time: 2 hours   **Cooking Time:** 0   **Servings: 4**

Ingredients:

- ✓ 4 cups flour
- ✓ 1 small potato, boiled, peeled, and mashed
- ✓ 6 tbsp s lukewarm water
- ✓ ½ cup pale lager

Directions:

- ❖ Allow the yeast to dissolve in the water.

- ❖ In a large mixing bowl, combine the flour, mashed potato, yeast mixture and beer; mix thoroughly. As a loose dough starts to form, add the oil and salt. Once the dough begins to pull away from the sides of the bowl, place on a floured work surface and knead until elastic.

Ingredients:

- ✓ 2 tbsp s dry active yeast
- ✓ 3 tbsp s extra virgin olive oil
- ✓ Salt, to taste

- ❖ Place the dough in an oiled bowl and cover it using a plastic wrap. In a warm spot, let the dough rise for about 2 hours or until it doubles in the size.

- ❖ Note that this dough tends to bake a little longer than others so be sure not to take it out too soon!

13) HEART SHAPED PIZZA

Preparation Time: 30 minutes　　**Cooking Time:** 20 minutes　　**Servings: 1**

Ingredients:

- ✓ 1 cup water
- ✓ 2 tablespoons milk
- ✓ 2 tsps sugar
- ✓ 1 1/4 tsp salt
- ✓ 1 tbsp shortening

Directions:

- ❖ Place water, milk, sugar, salt, shortening and olive oil in bowl of food processor and pulse to dissolve sugar and salt.

- ❖ Add yeast, semolina or corn meal, bread flour and all purpose flour. Process until a soft ball forms. Remove from machine and allow to rest, covered with a towel, about 45 minutes. OR to make by hand: Use only all-purpose flour. Place water, milk, sugar, salt, shortening and olive oil in bowl and dissolve sugar and salt.

Ingredients:

- ✓ 1 tablespoon olive oil
- ✓ 1 tablespoon durum semolina (or corn meal)
- ✓ 1 cup unbleached all-purpose flour
- ✓ 2 cups unbleached bread flour
- ✓ 1 1/4 tsp yeast

- ❖ Stir in yeast, semolina or corn meal, all purpose flour and knead to form a soft, but not-too sticky dough (8-10 minutes). Allow to rest, covered with a towel about 45 minutes.

- ❖ Deflate dough very gently before using and allow it to rest 15 minutes more before using in a recipe. You may refrigerate dough in an oiled plastic bag for up to two days.

- ❖ Shape dough into a heart. Top with your favorite sauce and toppings. Bake in a hot oven 425 - 450°F. for 15 -20 minutes.

14) HEART SHAPED VALENTINE PIZZA

Preparation Time: 30 minutes　　**Cooking Time:** 20 minutes　　**Servings: 1**

Ingredients:

- ✓ 1 large Pizza shell; pre-baked
- ✓ 1/3 cup Pizza sauce
- ✓ 1/3 cup Mozzarella or Jack cheese; grated
- ✓ 12 large Shrimp; cooked

Directions:

- ❖ Trim the pizza shell(s) or foccacia bread into heart shape, place on pizza pan or baking sheet. Spread
- ❖ pizza sauce on shell to near edge.
- ❖ Sprinkle cheese over sauce, not quite to edge of sauce. Place shrimp, in pairs, tails touching, to make hearts, on top of cheese

Ingredients:

- ✓ 1 medium Red Bell Pepper
- ✓ 3 Pieces artichoke hearts; frozen and thawed, sliced
- ✓ Olive oil
- ✓ Minced Basil

- ❖ Do the same with some slices of red bell pepper, using the top, where it
- ❖ curves, for the top of the heart. Put a few slices of artichoke heart here and there. drizzle a little olive
- ❖ oil over top. Sprinkle with minced basil (optional).
- ❖ Bake at 375^ degrees until cheese melts and pizza is piping hot. Serve hot

15) HEARTSHAPED MOZZARELLA AND FONTINA PIZZA

Preparation Time: 30 minutes   **Cooking Time:** 20 minutes   **Servings: 2**

Ingredients:
- ✓ 1 (10 oz.) can refrigerated pizza crust
- ✓ 4 tsp butter, divided
- ✓ 1/2 red pepper, thinly sliced
- ✓ 1 leek, cut into 1-inch strips
- ✓ 1 boneless, skinless chicken breast half, cut into small cubes

Directions:
- ❖ Preheat oven to 425°F. Unroll refrigerated pizza dough into rectangle or sq uare shape. Create a heart shape template out of paper towels or cardboard. Place template on dough and cut around heart shape using scissors. Place heart-shaped dough on greased cookie sheet and follow instructions on dough can for prebaking pizza crust. Set crust aside.

Ingredients:
- ✓ 1/4 cup pesto
- ✓ artichoke hearts, coarsely chopped, to taste
- ✓ 4 ounces Fontina cheese, shredded
- ✓ 1/2 cup mozzarella cheese, shredded
- ✓ 1/2 tsp dried oregano

- ❖ Saute red pepper and leeks in half of the butter until almost tender. Remove from skillet. Add chicken and other half of the butter to skillet and cook until chicken is done and lightly browned.
- ❖ Spread pesto over prebaked pizza crust. Top with sautéed leeks, red peppers, and chicken. Add artichoke hearts. Top with cheeses and bake at 425°F. for 7 to 10 minutes. Sprinkle with oregano.

16) HOMEMADE PIZZA

Preparation Time: 30 minutes   **Cooking Time:** 20 minutes   **Servings: 1**

Ingredients:
Dough
- ✓ 1 package Active Dry Yeast
- ✓ 1 cup Warm Water (105 to 115 degrees)
- ✓ 1 tsp Sugar
- ✓ 1 tsp Salt
- ✓ 2 tablespoons Oil
- ✓ 2 1/2 cups Flour
Sauce
- ✓ 1/2 cup chopped Onion
- ✓ oz.) can Tomato Sauce
- ✓ 1/4 tsp Salt

Directions:
- ❖ Dough:
- ❖ Dissolve yeast in warm water. Stir in remaining dough ingredients. Beat vigorously, about 20 strokes.
- ❖ C over bowl, allow dough to rest about 15 minutes, or until you have prepared sauce. Sauce:
- ❖ Mix sauce ingredients, set aside. Heat Oven to 425 degrees
- ❖ Divide dough in half. On lightly greased 12" pizza pans sprinkled with a light coating of corn meal, pat each half of dough out into a 10 to 12 inch circle on pizza pans. Divide sauce evenly between to pizza crusts and spread out.
- ❖ Sprinkle each pizza with 1/4 cup shredded Parmesan Cheese. Sprinkle each pizza with 2 tsp. dried Oregano Leaves.

Ingredients:
- ✓ 1 1/8 tsp bottled Garlic, or more to taste
- ✓ 1/8 tsp White Pepper
  Meat And Vegetable Toppings
- ✓ 1 cup sliced Pepperoni
- ✓ 1 cup chopped Onion s
- ✓ 1 cup frozen Birdseye Stir-fried Peppers
- ✓ 1 (4oz.) can sliced Mushrooms
- ✓ 1 cup sliced Ripe Olives
- ✓ 1 pound Sweet or Hot Italian Sausage, removed from casings

- ❖ Meat And Vegetable Toppings:
- ❖ Saute' sausage until almost done, stirring to break up. Add the peppers, onions, mushrooms, olives and pepperoni and continue cooking until sausage is completely done. Dump the skillet full of
- ❖ cooked toppings in a colander to drain. Drain very well.
- ❖ Sprinkle toppings evenly onto tops of pizzas. Sprinkle 1 cup shredded Mozzarella Cheese on each of
- ❖ the pizzas. Bake 20 to 25 minutes on lower rack of oven at 425 degrees until crust is brown and filling is hot and bubbly.

17) HOMEMADE PIZZA

Preparation Time: 30 minutes   **Cooking Time:** 20 minutes   **Servings: 1**

Ingredients:

- ✓ 1 1/4 ounce active baker's yeast
- ✓ 1 tsp sugar
- ✓ 1 1/4 cup warm water (110-115 degrees)
- ✓ 1/4 cup vegetable oil
- ✓ 1 tsp salt
- ✓ 3 1/2 cups all-purpose flour
- ✓ 1/2 pound ground beef

Directions:

- ❖ In large bowl, dissolve yeast and sugar in water; let stand for 5 min. Add oil and salt. Stir in flour, a cup at a time, to form soft dough. Turn onto floured board; knead until smooth and elastic, about 2-3 min. Place in greased bowl, tuning once to grease top. Cover and let rise in a warm place until doubled, about 45 min.

Ingredients:

- ✓ 1 small onion -chopped
- ✓ 15 ounces tomato sauce
- ✓ 1 tbsp dried oregano
- ✓ 1 tsp dried basil
- ✓ 1 medium green pepper -- diced
- ✓ 2 cups mozzarella cheese -- shredded

- ❖ Meanwhile, brown beef and onion; drain. Punch dough down; divide in half. Press each into a greased 12" pizza pan. Combine the tomato sauce, oregano and basil; spread over each crust. Top with beef mixture, green pepper and cheese. Bake at 400 degrees for 25-30 minutes or until crust is lightly browned.

18) HOT 'N SWEET PIZZA

Preparation Time: 30 minutes   **Cooking Time:** 20 minutes   **Servings: 1**

Ingredients:

- ✓ ounce size) round pre-baked thin crust Italian bread shell
- ✓ 1 can (8-ounce size) pizza sauce
- ✓ 1 can (8-ounce size) can pineapple tidbits in juice, well-drained
- ✓ 1 package (6-ounce size) Canadian bacon slices, quartered

Directions:

- ❖ Heat oven to 400°F. Place bread shell on large ungreased baking sheet. Spread pizza sauce evenly over shell; top with all remaining ingredients.

Ingredients:

- ✓ 2 tbsp seeded jalapeño chiles (or to taste)
- ✓ 3/4 cup shredded cheddar cheese
- ✓ 3/4 cup shredded mozzarella cheese

- ❖ Bake for 8 to 10 minutes or until cheese is melted and ingredientsare heated through.
- ❖ To serve, cut into wedges.

19) HOT DOG PIZZA

Preparation Time: 30 minutes   **Cooking Time:** 20 minutes   **Servings: 1**

Ingredients:

- ✓ 2 English muffins, split
- ✓ 2 hot dogs, each cut into 12 slices

Directions:

- ❖ Heat oven to 350. Place muffin halves cut side up on ungreased pan. Top each with 1 tablespoon tomato soup

Ingredients:

- ✓ 1/4 cup condensed tomato soup
- ✓ 1/4 cup shredded cheddar cheese

- ❖ Arrange 6 hot dog slices on each muffin half, sprinkle with 1 tbsp shredded cheddar cheese bake for 8-10 minutes our until cheese melts.

20) IMPOSSIBLE PIZZA

Preparation Time: 30 minutes   **Cooking Time:** 20 minutes   **Servings: 1**

Ingredients:

CRUST
- ✓ 2 tablespoons Cheese, parmesan, grated
- ✓ 1 cup Milk
- ✓ 2 Eggs
- ✓ 1/2 cup Bisq uick

TOPPINGS
- ✓ 1/2 cup Prego

Ingredients:
- ✓ Sausage; or ground meat
- ✓ Onions, chopped
- ✓ Bell peppers, chopped
- ✓ 2 tbsp Cheese, parmesan, grated
- ✓ 3/4 cup Cheese, mozzarella, shredded

Directions:

- ❖ Heat oven to 425. Grease a pie plate. Sprinkle onion and Parmesan cheese in pie plate. Beat milk, eggs, and bisq uick 15 seconds in blender on high.

- ❖ Pour into pie plate. Bake 20 minutes. 2. Spread pizza sauce over top. Top with remaining ingredients. Bake 10-15 minutes, until cheese is light brown.
- ❖ Cool 15 minutes.

21) INDIVIDUAL PESTO PIZZAS WITH MUSHROOMS AND OLIVES RECIPE

Preparation Time: 30 minutes   **Cooking Time:** 20 minutes   **Servings: 1**

Ingredients:
- ✓ 1/4 cup prepared pesto
- ✓ 8 Baked Individual Pizza Crusts
- ✓ 8 large Spinach leaves, trimmed
- ✓ 1/2 cup pizza sauce

Ingredients:
- ✓ 1/2 cup Nonfat mozzarella cheese, shredded
- ✓ 6 small Mushrooms, thinly sliced
- ✓ 5 Black olives, thinly sliced
- ✓ 1 tablespoon Parmesan cheese, freshly grated
- ❖ Finish with a light sprinkling of the Parmesan cheese.
- ❖ Place the pizzas on a cookie sheet and bake for 10 minutes.

Directions:

- ❖ Spray 1/2 tbsp of the pesto on each of the pizza crusts. Lay a spinach leaf on top and cover with 1 tbsp of the pizza sauce. Over the sauce, scatter 1 tbsp of mozzarella cheese, then eq ual amounts of the sliced mushrooms and olives.

22) KID SIZED PIZZA

Preparation Time: 30 minutes   **Cooking Time:** 20 minutes   **Servings: 1**

Ingredients:
- ✓ 4 English muffins, split
- ✓ 3/4 cup pizza sauce
- ✓ 1/4 pound Canadian Bacon;
- ✓ 6 large mushrooms, sliced
- ✓ 4 large black olives, sliced

Ingredients:
- ✓ 1 smallonion, sliced
- ✓ 1/2 medium green pepper, sliced
- ✓ 1/4 pound mozzarella cheese, shredded
- ✓ 1/3 cup parmesan cheese, grated
- ❖ Place on nonstick baking sheet. Bake at 350f for 10 to 15 minutes or until cheese melts and begins to brown. Serve hot.

Directions:

- ❖ On each muffin half, spread 2 tbsp pizza sauce. Top each with one-eighth of the Canadian bacon, mushrooms, olives, onion and green pepper.
- ❖ Sprinkle each with mozzarella and parmesan cheese, dividing equally.

23) KID SIZED SOUTHWEST PIZZA

Preparation Time: 30 minutes **Cooking Time:** 20 minutes **Servings: 1**

Ingredients:
- ✓ 6 pita bread rounds
- ✓ 16 ounces can refried beans
- ✓ 4 ounces chopped green chilies drained
- ✓ 1/2 cup diced tomato

Directions:
- ❖ Preheat oven to 400F degrees. Place pita rounds on a large greased baking sheet. Bake 8 minutes or until crisp, turning after 4 minutes. Let cool slightly. Combine beans and chilies mixing well. Spread about 1/3 cup bean mixture over each pita round. Divide tomato evenly among pizzas.

Ingredients:
- ✓ 3/4 cup shredded cheese
- ✓ 1 1/2 cup shredded iceberg lettuce
- ✓ 6 tablespoons sour cream

- ❖ Sprinkle with cheese. Bake 8 minutes longer or until mixture is hot and cheese melts. Remove from the oven. Top each pizza with 1/4 cup lettuce and 1 tablespoon sour cream.

24) LEEK TOMATO GOAT CHEESE PIZZA

Preparation Time: 30 minutes **Cooking Time:** 20 minutes **Servings: 1**

Ingredients:
- ✓ 1 1/2 tbsp Butter
- ✓ 2 med. leeks, thinly sliced
- ✓ 1 tbsp fresh parsley, minced

Directions:
- ❖ Melt butter in large skillet over medium-low heat. Add leeks; saute until tender, about 10 minutes. Season with salt and pepper. Stir in parsley. Cool. Spread leek topping evenly over pizza shell; sprinkle tomatoes over

Ingredients:
- ✓ 3/4 cup tomato, chopped
- ✓ 3 ounces Montrachet or Feta, crumbled
- ✓ 2 tablespoons olive oil
- ❖ Top with cheese. Drizzle 1 tbsp oil over. Bake about 10 minutes at 450 F. Remove from oven and brush crust with olive oil.

25) TYROLEAN PIZZA

Preparation Time: 30 minutes   **Cooking Time:** 15 minutes   **Servings: 4**

Ingredients:

For the pizzas
- ✓ 1 tsp Sugar
- ✓ 12 g Brewer's yeast
- ✓ 500 g 00 flour
- ✓ 3 tbsp. Extra virgin olive oil
- ✓ 250-300 mL Warmed water
- ✓ 2 tsps Salt

Directions:

- ❖ Classic Mixture
- ❖ On a pastry board, arrange the flour and give it a shape of the classic fountain.
- ❖ On the outermost edge of the flour, that where you should put the salt.
- ❖ Smash the brewer's yeast and dissolve it in 100 mL of warm water together with the sugar. Pour the mixture in the center of the fountain after adding the oil.
- ❖ Use your fingertips to begin working on the dough. Incorporate the flour gradually to the fountain edge. Add the necessary lukewarm water gradually and in a circular motion.
- ❖ From the edge, include more and more flour until elastic, soft and smooth dough forms at the center.
- ❖ On a floured surface, vigorously work on the dough until it doesn't stick on your hands anymore.

- ❖ Mixture with the Planetary Mixer
- ❖ In a planetary mixer with a mounted hook, insert the flour and add yeast, oil and 150 mL of water.
- ❖ At medium-low speed, knead for 5 minutes and also adding the rest of the water flush.
- ❖ Again, knead for 5 minutes, add salt and keep cooking for more 5 minutes until you obtain elastic, smooth and homogenous dough.

- ❖ How to make Tyrolean Pizza
- ❖ Form a ball with the dough that has been prepared using a planetary mixer or by hand and use a cloth to cover after making a cross cut.
- ❖ In a draft free and warm place, leave the dough to rise until it doubles in volume for about 2 hours

Ingredients:

For the dressing
- ✓ Fresh ground oregano to taste
- ✓ 1 Medium golden onion
- ✓ 1 tsp sugar
- ✓ 250 g Tomato sauce
- ✓ 400 g Mozzarella, well drained
- ✓ 250 g Speck, cut into thin slices
- ✓ 2 packs of pork frankfurters

- ❖ Divide the dough into 4 loaves once its volume doubles and put them in a container with a well-floured container, with a lid.
- ❖ Allow the dough to rise. This takes a couple of hours then go to the pizza Directions, one at a time.
- ❖ Sprinkle the first loaf with flour and put it on a lightly greased round pan. For beginners, you can use a drizzle of oil to first moisten the fingertips.
- ❖ Lightly press on the dough using your fingers so as to give it a circular shape.
- ❖ Make a movement that goes from the center to the edge when handling the pizza so as to push the gas bubbles, which are formed after the rising process towards the cornice. You should not flatten the latter as it must be crisp and high at the end of the cooking.
- ❖ Before baking the pizzas, preheat the oven for 30 minutes at 250 degrees. Then go to preparing the seasoning, which will be divided in 4 portions. Slice the onions thinly after peeling and rinsing them.
- ❖ For 2 minutes, blanch the frankfurters and then cut them in thin slices. In a bowl, put the tomato sauce and do the seasoning with 2 tbsp of oregano, salt, pepper and oil and also cut the mozzarella into long slices that are thin. Spread ¼ of the tomato sauce for the first pizza using the back of a spoon. In succession, distribute the frankfurters, onions and mozzarella.
- ❖ Use oil to wet the pizza surface and place it in an already hot oven. Since the pizza must cook more below than above, put the pan near the oven bottom.
- ❖ Allow the Tyrolean pizza to cook until the cornice has become golden and crispy and the pizza bottom is dry. This will take 13-15 minutes. Raise the bottom to see if the pizza is cooked.
- ❖ Remove the Tyrolean pizza from the oven when it finishes cooking, transfer it to a plate and then use speck slices to garnish it.
- ❖ You can now serve the freshly baked Tyrolean pizza.

26) BOSCAIOLA PIZZA

Preparation Time: 10 minutes   **Cooking Time:** 15 minutes   **Servings: 4**

Ingredients:

- ✓ 200 g Sausage
- ✓ 130 g Mozzarella
- ✓ Extra virgin olive oil to taste
- ✓ 400 g Pizza dough

Ingredients:

- ✓ Black pepper to taste
- ✓ 150 g Champignon mushrooms
- ✓ Salt to taste

Directions:

- ❖ Begin with preparing the pizza dough. Leave the dough to rise as you take care of the rest of the things. Clean and then cut the mushrooms into thin slices and then do the seasoning with pepper and a pinch of salt.

- ❖ Grease a 30 cm pan with a drizzle of oil to avoid the pizza from sticking and dice the mozzarella.

- ❖ Spread the dough in the pan directly once it is ready using your hands. Sprinkle with slices of champignon and diced mozzarella. Lastly, lay the sausage that is crumbled in small pieces and if desired, sprinkle with other oil.

- ❖ Preheat a static oven at 250 degrees and put the dough for 12-15 minutes. It is recommended to put the pan in the lower part of the oven and not in the center exactly and also check the times according to the appliance you are using.

- ❖ Take the boscaiola pizza out, cut and serve it. You can also accompany it with a nice beer.

27) CALZONE

Preparation Time: 40 minutes   **Cooking Time:** 10 minutes   **Servings: 6**

Ingredients:

- ✓ 500 g 0 flour
- ✓ 25 g Brewer's yeast, Fresh
- ✓ 300 mL water
- ✓ 1 tsp Sugar
- ✓ 30 g Extra virgin olive oil
- ✓ 10 g Salt
  For the classic filling
- ✓ 60 g Ham, cooked
- ✓ 10 g Extra virgin olive oil
- ✓ 60 g Mozzarella
- ✓ 100 g Tomato puree

Directions:

- ❖ Begin with dough Directions following the procedure. In a warm and dry place, allow it to rise for at least 2 hours until the dough doubles.
- ❖ When the dough rises, begin the Directions of vegetables filling through washing and shredding them finely in various vegetable varieties like pepper, carrots, aubergines and zucchini.
- ❖ In a pan, put a spoonful of oil, salt and pepper and on high heat, sauté them for few minutes. On the colander, put the mozzarella that has been cut into cubes for it to lose the excess water.

Ingredients:

- ✓ Salt to taste
- ✓
- ✓ Ingredients for the vegetarian filling
- ✓ 50 g Courgettes
- ✓ 50 g Red peppers
- ✓ 60 g Mozzarella
- ✓ 50 g Carrots
- ✓ 50 g Eggplants
- ✓ Black pepper to taste
- ✓ 10 g Extra virgin olive oil
- ✓ Salt to taste

- ❖ Cut the mozzarella well into cubes, drain it very well and then ham into small pieces. Use oil, 100 mL of tomato sauce and salt to do the seasoning, this is for the classic filling.
- ❖ On a work surface, roll out the dough high 2mm and 18 cm wide rectangles; put the filling in small piles that are arranged in the rectangle center.
- ❖ On one side, lift the dough and cover the overlapping filling on the other side. Use a glass or 10 cm diameter pastry cutter and cut half-moon breeches and use the fork edges to press on the side to be glued.
- ❖ Use oil to lightly brush the mini shoes and in a fan, oven heated at 230 degrees, bake for 10 to 15 minutes.
- ❖ These mini-baked shoes will be served hot but be very careful and not burn yourself with the filling.

28) PEKING DUCK PIZZA RECIPE

Preparation Time: 45 minutes   **Cooking Time:** 25 minutes   **Servings: 4**

Ingredients:

- ✓ 1 pound boneless duck breast -skin on
- ✓ 2 tbsp hoisin sauce
- ✓ 10 small won-ton wrappers -cut 1/2 inch strips
- ✓ 1 cup olive oil -for frying
- ✓ 2 pizza crusts (9 inch size)

Ingredients:

- ✓ cornmeal (to dust pan)
- ✓ 1/4 cup hoisin sauce
- ✓ 1 1/2 cup mozzarella cheese -shredded
- ✓ 8 scallions -white part only, slivered
- ✓ 2 cups mushrooms (white, oyster and shitake)

Directions:

- ❖ Bake duck which has been coated with hoisin sauce and chill. Cut into 1/8 inch slices. Fry won ton strips in hot olive oil (375 degrees) until brown and crisp. Drain and set aside. Sauté mushrooms in one tablespoon olive oil and set aside. Make or use purchased pizza dough (two 9 inch rounds).

- ❖ Spread 1 to 2 tsps of hoisin sauce over the dough.

- ❖ Cover with the mozzarella, slivered green onions and sliced duck. Spread the sautéed mushrooms over duck.

- ❖ Bake (preferably on a pizza stone) at 500 degrees for 9 to 10 minutes or until cheese is bubbly. Slice the pizza and then top with the won tons and drizzle on more hoisin sauce in a spider web pattern.

29) PEPERONATA AND SAUSAGE PIZZA RECIPE

Preparation Time: 45 minutes   **Cooking Time:** 25 minutes   **Servings: 4**

Ingredients:

- ✓ Cornmeal for dusting
- ✓ 12 ounces Whole-Wheat Pizza Dough or other prepared dough
- ✓ 1 link Italian turkey sausage, casing removed
- ✓ Peperonata
- ✓ 3 tsps extra-virgin olive oil, divided
- ✓ 1 cup slivered onion
- ✓ 1 cup thinly sliced red bell pepper
- ✓ 2 cloves garlic, minced

Ingredients:

- ✓ 1/8 tsp crushed red pepper
- ✓ 3/4 cup diced tomato
- ✓ 2 tsp red-wine vinegar
- ✓ 1/8 tsp salt
- ✓ Freshly ground pepper to taste
- ✓ 1 cup grated part-skim mozzarella cheese
- ✓ 1/4 cup freshly grated Parmesan cheese

Directions:

- ❖ Place a pizza stone or inverted baking sheet on the lowest oven rack preheat oven to 500°F or highest setting.

- ❖ 2. inch pizza pan with cooking spray and dust with cornmeal. Cook sausage in a small nonstick skillet over medium heat, turning from time to time, until browned and cooked through, 10 to 12 minutes. Drain and cut into 1/4-inchthick slices.

- ❖ Meanwhile, prepare peperonata: Heat 2 tsp oil in a large nonstick skillet over medium heat. Add onion and bell pepper; cook, stirring often, until softened, 4 to 6 minutes. Add garlic and crushed red pepper; cook, stirring, for 1 minute. Add tomato and cook for 3 minutes. Remove from the heat and stir in vinegar, salt and pepper.

- ❖ Transfer to a plate and let cool. On a lightly floured surface, roll the dough into a 13-inch circle.

- ❖ Transfer to the prepared pan. Turn edges under to make a slight rim. Brush the rim with the remaining 1 tsp oil.

- ❖ Sprinkle mozzarella over the crust, leaving a 1/2-inch border. Top with the peperonata and sausage. Sprinkle with parmesan. Place the pizza pan on the heated pizza stone (or baking sheet) and bake the pizza until the bottom is crispand golden, 10 to 14 minutes. Serve immediately.

30) PHILLY CHEESE STEAK CRESCENT PIZZA

Preparation Time: 45 minutes   **Cooking Time:** 25 minutes   **Servings: 4**

Ingredients:

- ✓ 1 can (8-oz. size) refrigerated crescent rolls
- ✓ 8 ounces thinly sliced cooked deli roast beef
- ✓ 1 tablespoon purchased Italian salad dressing
- ✓ 1 1/2 cup shredded mozzarella cheese

Ingredients:

- ✓ 2 tablespoons olive or vegetable oil
- ✓ 1 cup coarsely chopped green bell pepper
- ✓ 1 cup coarsely chopped onions
- ✓ 1/2 tsp beef-flavor instant bouillon

Directions:

- ❖ Heat oven to 375 F. Unroll dough in ungreased 13x9-inch pan. Press over bottom and 1/2 inch up
- ❖ sides. FirmLy press perforations to seal.
- ❖ Wrap beef tightly in foil. Place crescent dough and beef in oven.
- ❖ Bake at 375 F. for 10 minutes or until crust is light golden brown.
- ❖ Arrange warm beef over partially baked crust. Brush with salad dressing.

- ❖ Sprinkle with cheese. Return to oven; bake an additional 8 to 10 minutes or until edges of crust are golden brown and cheese is melted.
- ❖ Meanwhile, heat oil in medium skillet over medium heat until hot. Add bell pepper, onions and bouillon; cook and stir 3 to 5 minutes or until tender, stirring freq uently. Spoon cooked vegetables over melted cheese.

31) PITA PESTO PIZZA

Preparation Time: 45 minutes   **Cooking Time:** 25 minutes   **Servings: 4**

Ingredients:

- ✓ 2 cloves garlic
- ✓ 1/2 cup lightly packed parsley
- ✓ 4 cups torn spinach
- ✓ 1/2 cup grated parmesan
- ✓ 1 1/2 tablespoon dried whole basil

Ingredients:

- ✓ 1 tbsp lemon juice
- ✓ 2 (6 inch size) whole wheat pitas
- ✓ 1 cup chopped red bell pepper
- ✓ 1/2 cup shredded part-skim mozzarella cheese

Directions:

- ❖ Position knife blade in processor. Drop garlic and parsley through Food chute with processor running; process 15 seconds or until minced. Add spinach, parmesan, basil and lemon juice; process 30 seconds. Scrape bowl with rubber spatula and process an additional 30 seconds or until smooth.

- ❖ Split pita breads into 4 rounds, spread 2 Tbsp. Spinach Mixture over interior of each pita round. Top with bell pepper and Cheese. Bake at 450 for 5 min. Or until cheese melts. Serve warm.

32) PITA PIZZA

Preparation Time: 45 minutes   **Cooking Time:** 25 minutes   **Servings: 4**

Ingredients:

- ✓ 1 ounce lowfat mozzarella cheese -shredded
- ✓ 1 pita bread
- ✓ sun-dried tomato halves -rehydrated with water and chopped

Directions:

- ❖ Shred low-fat mozzarella onto pita round, add sun-dried tomatoes, marinated artichoke heart, snips of fresh basil and a bottled red pepper or, thinly slice a fresh red pepper. Broil until hot and bubbly.

Ingredients:

- ✓ 1 marinated artichoke heart -rinsed and drained
- ✓ chopped or sliced fresh basil
- ✓ red pepper -hot or mild, fresh or roasted

❖

33) Pita Pizza For One Recipe

Ingredients:

- ✓ 3 ounces lean ground beef
- ✓ 2 tablespoons chopped green pepper
- ✓ 2 tablespoons canned chopped mushrooms
- ✓ 2 tablespoons pizza sauce

Directions:

- ❖ In a small skillet, cook the ground beef and green pepper till meat is brown and green pepper is tender. Drain off fat. Stir mushrooms, pizza sauce, and oregano into skillet. Cook and stir about 1 minute or till meat mixture is heated through.

Ingredients:

- ✓ 1/8 tsp dried oregano, crushed
- ✓ 1 large pita bread round, split horizontally
- ✓ Crushed red pepper (optional)
- ✓ 1 tablespoon shredded mozzarella cheese

❖ Spread meat mixture over one pita bread half. (Store remaining pita bread half for another use.) Sprinkle with crushed red pepper, if desired. Top with shredded cheese. Place pita bread on a baking sheet. Broil 3 to 4 inches from heat about 2 minutes or till cheese melts.

34) YUMMY PIZZA

Preparation Time: 45 minutes   **Cooking Time:** 25 minutes   **Servings: 4**

Ingredients:

Pizza Crust
- ✓ 5 1/2 cups all-purpose flour, as needed
- ✓ 2 cups warm water (110F - 115F)
- ✓ 1/4 cup olive oil
- ✓ 2 packages yeast
- ✓ 2 tsps of salt
- ✓ yellow cornmeal
- ✓ SAUCE
- ✓ 29 ounces whole peeled tomatoes, undrained

Ingredients:
- ✓ 2 tbsp olive oil
- ✓ 2 medium onion, chopped
- ✓ 2 clove garlic, minced
- ✓ 4 tbsp tomato paste
- ✓ 2 tsps crushed, dried oregano leaves
- ✓ 2 tsps crushed dried basil leaves
- ✓ 1 tsp sugar
- ✓ 1 tsp salt

Directions:

- ❖ For crust, proof yeast with slat in warm water. Mix yeast, water and olive oil, stir in flour 1 cup at a time. Turn out onto floured surface, knead until smooth, 5 to 7 minute, adding flour as necessary. Dough will be soft. Place in oiled bowl, turning to coat all sides, cover with plastic wrap and let rise in warm place until doubled. Punch down and let rest 15 mins. Divide in half an, press out into two 12 inch round pizza pans or 10x15x1 pans or 1 of each. sprinkled with yellow cornmeal(prevents crust from sticking).

- ❖ For sauce, finely chop tomatoes in can with knife, reserving juice. Heat olive oil in medium saucepan over medium heat. Add onion, cook 5 minutes or until soft. Add garlic, cook 30 sec. More Add tomatoes with liq uid, tomato paste, oregano, basil, 1/2-tsp sugar, 1/2-tsp salt and black pepper. Bring to boil over high heat. Reduce heat to medium-low. Simmer, uncovered 10-15 minutes until thickened. Stirring occasionally.

35) CROCKPOT PIZZA

Preparation Time: 45 minutes   **Cooking Time:** 25 minutes   **Servings: 4**

Ingredients:
- ✓ 2 pounds ground beef browned and drained
- ✓ 2 pounds grated Mozzarella cheese
- ✓ 1 onion, chopped
- ✓ 1 package (whole) pepperoni, sliced
- ✓ 1 box rigatoni noodles, cooked

Ingredients:
- ✓ 2 cans cream of mushroom soup
- ✓ 2 (4 oz.) cans mushrooms
- ✓ 1 can black olives
- ✓ 2 cans pizza sauce

Directions:

- ❖ Alternate layers in crock pot as follows: hamburger, noodles, cheese, soup, mushrooms and olives, onions, sauce and pepperoni. Heat on low in crock pot for 4 hours.

36) PIZZA WITH MORTADELLA AND BUFFALO MOZZARELLA

Preparation Time: 30 minutes   **Cooking Time:** 12 minutes   **Servings: 2**

Ingredients:

- ✓ 500 g 0 Flour
- ✓ 300 g Water
- ✓ 1 g Fresh brewer's yeast
- ✓ 12 g Salt
- ✓ 1 tbsp. Extra virgin olive oil

Ingredients:

To stuff
- ✓ 100 g Mortadella
- ✓ 200 g Buffalo mozzarella
- ✓ Basil to taste
- ✓ Extra virgin olive oil to taste

Directions:

- ❖ To make this pizza with mortadella and buffalo mozzarella, begin by taking care of the dough. In a mixer with a hook, pour in the flour, add yeast and slowly pour the water as you begin working on the dough.

- ❖ Knead the dough and when it begins to string, add salt and water and then keep adding gradually. Add the oil once all the oil has been absorbed completely. Continue kneading the dough until it absorbs that too and starts stringing around the hook.

- ❖ When the dough is soft and smooth. Turn it over on a floured work surface and by rotating the dough between your hands, form a ball and then grease the bowl with oil and lay the dough there.

- ❖ Sprinkle the surface lightly using flour and use a cling film to cover the dough and allow it to rise for 10-12 hours at room temperature because the rising times vary according to the season.

- ❖ Turn the dough on a floured work surface when the leavening is over and divide them in two parts to form a ball and lay them on a kitchen towel. Let it rise until it doubles in the volume or for about 2 hours.

- ❖ Get a round baking pan with diameter of 32 cm and flour it. Using your hands to spread, put one of the balls in the center until the pan is covered completely and mind to leave the tallest cornice.

- ❖ Get the sheet you previously used to cover the pan. Proceed with the same process for the second pizza. Heat the oven that is possibly ventilated at 250 degrees and on the second track at the bottom, position the grill. Cut the mozzarella buffalo into slices and keep them aside.

- ❖ Season one of the pizzas with the oil necessary to grease the surface once the oven has reached the required temperature and cook for 7-8 minutes.

- ❖ Remove the pizza from the oven and fill it with half of the buffalo that was prepared. Again, bake it for 3-4 minutes, remove it from the oven and fill it with basil to taste and half of the mortadella and continue in the same way for the second pizza.

- ❖ Immediately serve your pizza with mortadella and buffalo.

37) MASCARPONE PIZZA, SPECK AND WALNUTS

Preparation Time: 15 minutes   **Cooking Time**: 30 minutes   **Servings: 4**

Ingredients:

- ✓ 60 g Extra virgin olive oil
- ✓ 600 g Water
- ✓ 1 kg 0 Flour
- ✓ 20 g Salt
- ✓ 7 g Dry brewer's yeast
  For the stuffing
- ✓ 10 g Extra virgin olive oil

Directions:

- ❖ To make the marinara pizza, begin by pouring the flour into a mixer bowl. Add 100 mL of water and yeast and then use a hook mounted at medium-low speed to operate the planetary mixer.

- ❖ Continue by adding water little at a time and make sure you wait till the previous dose is well absorbed by the flour. When you have added at least ¾ of water, keep kneading after adding salt. Always keep adding the rest of the water flush and allow it to work until you get a homogeneous and smooth mixture.

- ❖ Gradually add the oil at this point and remove the dough from the planetary mixer once the oil has absorbed completely and use your hands to shape it until you form a ball. Put it in a lightly greased bowl.

- ❖ Use a clean cloth or a cling film to cover and allow it to rise in the oven while lights are on. Hold on until the dough has doubled in its size but better if tripled and continue with the pizza Directions.

- ❖ Transfer the dough to a pastry board once it rises and divide it in 4 equal parts. Do this for each of the balls. Use a clean towel to cover and then let it stand for 30 minutes

Ingredients:

- ✓ 700 g Tomato sauce
- ✓ 150 g Creamy mascarpone
- ✓ 10 g Oregano
- ✓ 150 g Sliced speck
- ✓ 600 g Buffalo mozzarella or fiordilatte
- ✓ 40 g Walnut kernels
- ✓ Salt to taste
- ❖ .

- ❖ Grease 4 30 cm diameter pizza pans lightly using a drizzle of oil. In the center of the pan, that's where you should put the ball of the dough and begin squeezing from the center outwards if necessary, slightly pulling the sides.

- ❖ Set aside the pizza you are spreading and roll out another one and let the previous one rest if the dough is too elastic and is returning to the shape it had previously. Try spreading the dough over the entire tray surface.

- ❖ In a large bowl separately, pour the tomato sauce and season with oil, oregano and salt. On the pizza base, pour a generous tomato sauce ladle and let it cover almost the whole area by spreading it in a circular motion and leave a boarder of about 1.5 cm.

- ❖ Chop the mozzarella coarsely and put it on the pizza. With the help of a tsp, add the mascarpone.

- ❖ Allow the stuffed pizza to rest for at least 10 minutes and then bake for 15 minutes at 250 degrees in a static oven. Meanwhile, use a knife to lightly chop the nuts.

- ❖ Add the freshly chopped walnuts and speck slices onto the pizza once it's out of the oven. Serve the mascarpone speck and walnut pizza while still hot.

38) WALLET PIZZA WITH SALAMI

Preparation Time: 30 minutes   **Cooking Time**: 30 minutes   **Servings: 4**

Ingredients:

- ✓ 3 g Dry brewer's yeast
- ✓ 440 g Water at room temperature
- ✓ 750 g 0 Flour
- ✓ 20 g Salt
-     To season
- ✓ Oregano to taste

Directions:

- ❖ In preparing the pizza with salami, begin by making the pizza dough. In a mixer bowl, pour in the flour, and 100 mL of water and with a hook at medium-low speed, operate the mixer.

- ❖ Add water slowly by slowly and make sure you wait to add once the previous flour has been absorbed by the flour very well.

- ❖ Add salt and keep kneading once at least ¾ of water have been added. Keep adding the water flush and let it work until you get a homogeneous and smooth mixture.

- ❖ Take the dough out of the planetary at this point and work on it for few minutes on a flat surface so as to favor better the glutinic mesh and then use your hands to shape until you get a ball and put it in a slightly greased bowl.

- ❖ Use a clean towel or a cling film to cover the dough and put it in the oven with lights on at 26-30 degrees temperature as the maximum. Hold on until the dough at least doubles in the volume. This usually takes like 1 hour and 30 minutes and for it to triple, it takes like 2 to 3 hours.

- ❖ Transfer the dough on the pastry board and divide it in 4 equal parts one it rises. You can use a tarot. Using your hands, form small balls from each of these.

Ingredients:

- ✓ 200 g Spicy salami
- ✓ 750 g Mozzarella
- ✓ 10 g Salt
- ✓ 600 g Tomato pulp
- ✓ 30 g Extra virgin olive oil

- ❖ Use a clean cloth to cover once you have finished and again allow it rest for 30 minutes. Meanwhile, pour tomato sauce in a bowl and do the seasoning with oregano. Add salt and olive oil and when 30 minutes elapse, pick your dough and start rolling it out.

- ❖ On a floured surface, use your hands to lightly crush a ball and gently pull the dough until the thickness is at least 15 cm.

- ❖ Pass the pizza in a lightly greased pan at this point and use your hands to spread it to cover the whole surface.

- ❖ Distribute the passata on the pizzas, almost covering the whole area and spreading it in circular motion and only leave a boarder of 1.5 cm.

- ❖ In a static preheated oven, bake each pizza for 10 minutes at 250 degrees in the lowest part of the oven. Meanwhile, slice the salami and cut every slice in half.

- ❖ Take out each pizza and add pieces of salami and diced mozzarella. At the same temperature, bake again for 20 minutes and putting the pan in the central shelf of the oven.

- ❖ Take the pizzas out of the oven as soon as they are ready and while still hot, fold them, folding in half and then in half again like a booklet.

- ❖ Serve your pizza with hot salami.

39) FRIED PANZEROTTI

Preparation Time: 45 minutes   **Cooking Time:** 15 minutes   **Servings: 20**

Ingredients:

- ✓ 500 g 00 flour
- ✓ 15 g Extra virgin olive oil
- ✓ 20 g Coarse salt
- ✓ 7 g Dry brewer's yeast
- ✓ 570 g Lukewarm water
- ✓ 500 g Manitoba flour
- ✓ 10 g Sugar

Directions:

- ❖ In preparing the fried panzerotti, in a large bowl, mix the Manitoba flour and 00 flour. In a little warm water, dissolve the yeast taken from the total dose and also add the sugar.
- ❖ To the flour, add the dissolved yeast and in the water that has remained, melt the coarse salt and on the flour, pour the liquid flush and use your hands to begin mixing the ingredients. Mount the hook and knead at medium speed if you want to use the planetary mixer.
- ❖ Add the oil as well and vigorously mix. Transfer the dough to a pastry board and keep kneading and working on it until you get soft and smooth dough.
- ❖ You can now divide the dough in 20 parts of 80 g each and work on each and every part to form a ball and after that, put them on a tray or a pastry board where they are well spaced from each other.
- ❖ In an oven that is turned off and the lights are on, cover the dough with a blanket and cloth and let the balls rise until they double in the volume.

Ingredients:

For the stuffing:
- ✓ 200 g, Tomato sauce
- ✓ Oregano to taste
- ✓ 500 g Mozzarella
- ✓ Salt to taste

For frying:
- ✓ Seed oil to taste

- ❖ Meanwhile, prepare the panzerotti filling. In a bowl, mix the tomato puree and mozzarella together after cutting the mozzarella in small cubes. Salt and then season with oregano.
- ❖ In a large pot, heat the seed oil and start preparing the panzerotti once the balls have risen. Use a rolling pin to roll out every ball and give it a round shape with a diameter of approximately 20 cm. At the center, put a generous spoonful of filling.
- ❖ Seal the edges well and close the panzerotti that is forming a crescent by first applying pressure using your fingers and then folding the dough inwardly and lastly using the fork prongs, press in order to avoid the filling to come out during the cooking process.
- ❖ Dip the panzerotti immediately in boiling oil and turn them both sides until they become golden brown.
- ❖ Drain them on the paper towels and serve the fried panzerotti while they are still hot.

40) TROPICAL FOCACCIA

Preparation Time: 30 minutes   **Cooking Time:** 30 minutes   **Servings: 4**

Ingredients:

- ✓ 750 g of Plain Flour
- ✓ 280 mL of water
- ✓ 7 gr of dry yeast
- ✓ 1/2 tsp of malt (about 2 g)

Ingredients:

- ✓ 1 tbsp of salt (about 15 g)
- ✓ 2 eggs
- ✓ 100 g of unsalted butter

Directions:

- ❖ Dissolve 7 g of dry yeast and 1/2 tsp of malt in 280 mL of water;
- ❖ Start kneading by adding 750 g of flour a little at a time and 2 eggs one at a time;
- ❖ When the dough starts to compact, add 100 g of butter, 1 tbsp of salt and keep kneading;
- ❖ Divide it into 2 balls (one of 650 g and one of about 500 g) and let them rest for 2 hours;
- ❖ Start by rolling out the biggest dough ball, which will serve as a base, and place it on an oiled pan;
- ❖ Then, stretch the smaller dough ball, trying to give it the same shape and size as the previous one;
- ❖ Instead of stretch the smaller dough on a baking tin, stretch it on a sheet of baking paper and let it rise at room temperature, covered by cling film from any drafts, for about 4 hours;
- ❖ Then, spread the chopped pineapple, ham, and grated cheese on the first layer in the pan;

- ❖ Cover the remaining portion of the dough with the rest of the ingredients, helping yourself with baking paper so as not to ruin the leavening;
- ❖ Make incisions on the surface so that they act as a vent during cooking;
- ❖ Let it rise for an hour and a half at room temperature
- ❖ Bake at 230°C/450°F for 20/25 minutes.
- ❖ Recommended topping!
- ❖ For the stuffing:
- ❖ The recipe includes:
- ❖ 250 g of
- ❖ diced cooked ham
- ❖ 1 pineapple
- ❖ 250 g of
- ❖ grated Emmental

41) PINSA ROMANA

Preparation Time: 30 minutes   **Cooking Time:** 30 minutes   **Servings: 4**

Ingredients:

- ✓ For 2 pinsas:
- ✓ 200 g of Plain Flour
- ✓ 40 g of Buckwheat Flour
- ✓ 170 mL of water

Directions:

- ❖ Start by mixing 200 g of plain flour and 40 g of buckwheat flour;
- ❖ Dissolve 6 g of dry yeast in 170 mL of water and start kneading, adding the flours until the water is completely absorbed;
- ❖ Add 1 tsp of salt, 2 tbsp of oil and knead until you get a homogeneous and compact dough;
- ❖ Let the dough rest for about an hour, then divide it into two loaves;
- ❖ Place them in an airtight container with cornflour underneath and put them in the fridge for about 12 hours;
- ❖ Take it out of the fridge and let it acclimate for about 2 hours;
- ❖ Once the dough has doubled in volume, stretch the balls helping yourself with abundant cornflour, and press gently with your fingertips until you get an elongated and rounded shape of about 30/40 cm in length;

Ingredients:

- ✓ 6 g of dry yeast
- ✓ 2 tbsp of extra virgin olive oil (14 g)
- ✓ 1 heaped tsp of salt (about 7 g)
- ✓ Cornmeal flour q.s.

- ❖ Once the excess cornmeal has been removed, place the dough on the pan, top the pinsas, and bake them at 250°C/450°F for about 14 minutes.
- ❖ Recommended topping!
- ❖ Why not top this one with cheese fondue?
- ❖ Ingredients:
- ❖ 200 g of mozzarella
- ❖ 100 g of smoked provolone
- ❖ 500 g of brie
- ❖ 30 g of chopped pistachios
- ❖ 100 g of mortadella
- ❖ Once the pinsas have risen, top them with your chosen cheeses and bake them;
- ❖ Once cooked, add the mortadella and chopped pistachios

42) Pinsa Rome

Preparation Time: 30 minutes   **Cooking Time**: 30 minutes   **Servings: 4**

Ingredients:

- ✓ For 2 pinsas:
- ✓ 200 g of Very Strong Flour
- ✓ 30 g of Rice Flour
- ✓ 50 g of Plain Flour

Ingredients:

- ✓ 220 mL of water
- ✓ 2 g of dry yeast
- ✓ 1 heaped tsp of salt (about 7 g)

Directions:

- ❖ Dissolve 2 g of dry yeast in 220 mL of water;
- ❖ Mix 200 g of very strong flour, 50 g of plain flour, and 30 g of rice flour;
- ❖ Knead the flour mix with 1/3 of the water and yeast for a few minutes; Continue to knead, adding the second third of water a little at a time to help the absorption;
- ❖ Pause for 10 minutes to favor the autolysis of the dough, then add the remaining part of water and continue to knead until you get a homogeneous mixture;
- ❖ Make a series of folds every 20 minutes 5 times to reinforce the dough;
- ❖ Place it in an airtight container in the fridge for about 20 / 24h;
- ❖ Once the dough has been taken out from the fridge, divide it into two pieces of equal weight;
- ❖ Let the loaves rise on a thin layer of semolina flour for 6 hours at a temperature between 25 and 28°C/ 77° and 82°F;
- ❖ After the leavening time, stretch out the balls with the help of abundant semolina flour, pressing gently with your fingertips until you get an elongated and rounded shape of about 30/40 cm in length;
- ❖ Once the excess cornmeal has been removed, place the dough on the baking tray, topping the pinsa, and bake at 250°C/480°F for about 14 minutes.
- ❖ Recommended topping!
- ❖ Ingredients for a double starch topping:
- ❖ Potatoes
- ❖ Rosemary
- ❖ 125 g of mozzarella cheese
- ❖ 100 g of Stracchino (or cream)
- ❖ Extra virgin olive oil
- ❖ Cut the potatoes very thin and leave them to soak overnight to make them lose the starch;
- ❖ Once the dough has risen, season with stracchino (or cream) and pieces of mozzarella, cover the entire surface with the sliced potatoes, a drizzle of EVO oil, and a pinch of chopped rosemary, and salt.

43) FRIED SWEET PIZZA

Preparation Time: 30 minutes   **Cooking Time:** 30 minutes   **Servings: 4**

Ingredients:
- ✓ 270 g of Strong Flour
- ✓ 120 mL of water
- ✓ 60 mL of warm milk
- ✓ 6 g of fresh yeast

Ingredients:
- ✓ 1 level tsp of salt (about 3 g)
- ✓ 1 tsp of coconut oil (about 3g)
- ✓ Pistachio cream (see chapter 9)

Directions:
- ❖ Dissolve 4g of fresh yeast in 120 mL of water and 60 mL of warm milk;
- ❖ Start kneading by adding 270 g of strong flour a little at a time;
- ❖ Also, add 1 tsp of salt, 1 tsp of coconut oil (melted, almost at room temperature) and knead well until the dough is smooth and homogeneous;
- ❖ Cover the dough with cling film and let it rest for 1 hour.

- ❖ Divide the dough into two parts, form 2 loaves and let them rise until doubled (it will take 5/6 hours at 25°C/77°F);
- ❖ Fry the pizza in hot oil, flipping it on both sides;
- ❖ Dry it with paper towels then spread the pistachio cream on the pizza's surface and decorate it with white chocolate flakes.

44) SWEET PIZZA SPECIAL

Preparation Time: 30 minutes   **Cooking Time:** 30 minutes   **Servings: 4**

Ingredients:
- ✓ Biga:
- ✓ 260 g of strong flour
- ✓ 2 g of fresh yeast
- ✓ 120 mL of water
- ✓ Dough:
- ✓ 30 g of Plain Flour
- ✓ ½ tsp of sugar (about 2 g)
- ✓ 20 g of mother yeast

Ingredients:
- ✓ ½ tsp of salt (about 3 g)
- ✓ 1 tbsp of extra virgin olive oil (about 7 g)
- ✓ 25 mL of water
- ✓ a few drops of milk
- ✓ For the topping:
- ✓ Chantilly cream or hazelnut cream (see chapter 9)
- ✓ Chopped hazelnuts

Directions:
- ❖ Create the biga by dissolving 2 g of fresh active yeast in 120 mL of water, then add the flour, knead it, leaving the dough very rough and let it rest for about 16 hours at 20°C/68°F;
- ❖ The next day, dissolve 20 g of mother yeast in 25 mL of water and add it to the biga and the rest of the ingredients, adding salt as the last ingredient;
- ❖ Keep kneading it, until the dough reaches the dough point;

- ❖ Put the dough to rise for 2 hours and then proceed to make two balls of equal weight;
- ❖ Make the second leavening, which will last another 2 hours;
- ❖ Then stretch the dough balls, wet the top with a few drops of milk, prick the surface with a fork (to avoid creating a ball!), and proceed with baking it;
- ❖ Once the discs have cooled, spread your favorite cream on the surface and add a few chopped hazelnuts as a garnish.

45) SWEET PIZZA DELICIOUS

Preparation Time: 30 minutes   **Cooking Time:** 30 minutes   **Servings: 4**

Ingredients:

- ✓ 150 g of Very Strong Flour
- ✓ 80 g of Semolina Flour
- ✓ 70 mL of milk
- ✓ 70 mL of water
- ✓ 60 g of mother yeast
- ✓ 1/2 tsp of malt (about 3 g)

Ingredients:

- ✓ 1 level tsp of salt (about 2 g)
  Topping
- ✓ 150 mL of vanilla cream
- ✓ 1 Peach
- ✓ Almond flakes

Directions:

- ❖ Dissolve 60 g of yeast in a mixture of 70 mL of water, 70 mL of milk and 1 tsp of malt;
- ❖ Add 150 g of Manitoba, 80 g of Semolina and start kneading;
- ❖ Add 1 tsp of salt and knead it until you get a nice smooth and homogeneous dough;
- ❖ Place it in an airtight container and let it mature in the fridge for 12 hours;
- ❖ Remove the dough from the fridge and divide it into 2 dough ball;
- ❖ Once the dough has doubled in volume (it will take about 5 hours) stretch it and prick the surface with a fork so that you avoid ballooning during cooking;

- ❖ Proceed with cooking and, if you do not have a professional oven, I recommend that you proceed with the combined pan + grill cooking that you can find explained in chapter 1;
- ❖ Once golden-brown, take it out of the oven and top it with vanilla cream, peaches, and almond flakes.
- ❖ Tips!
- ❖ Another great topping idea:
- ❖ Mango jam (or any jam of your choice, the recipe is in chapter 9)
- ❖ 20 g of dehydrated coconut
- ❖ 20 g of white chocolate flakes

46) EVERYDAY PREP TIME: 30 MINUTES

Preparation Time: 30 minutes   **Cooking Time:** 30 minutes   **Servings: 4**

Ingredients:

- ✓ 180 g of Very Strong Flour
- ✓ 20 g of peanut flour
- ✓ 160 mL of water
- ✓ 60 g of mother yeast
- ✓ 1 tsp of peanut butter
- ✓ 3 g of salt (1/2 tsp)
- ✓ 1 handful of chopped peanuts

Ingredients:

- ✓ 1/2 tsp of malt (about 2 g)
  Topping:
- ✓ Hazelnut and chocolate cream (recipe in chapter 9)
- ✓ 100 g raspberry
- ✓ Marshmallows
- ✓ Icing sugar

Directions:

- ❖ Start by creating a pre-ferment, dissolving 60 g of mother yeast in half of the water (80mL) and adding 180g of very strong flour and 20g of peanut flour (if you have problems finding this flour, you can add the same weight of very strong flour and 1 tsp of peanut butter previously dissolved in water);
- ❖ Let the pre-ferment mature for about 1 hour at room temperature and then in the fridge for 12 hours;
- ❖ Take the dough out of the fridge and let it acclimate for about an hour;
- ❖ Add the remaining water (80mL), 1/2 tsp of malt, ½ of salt, 1 handful of peanuts and finish kneading;

- ❖ Make an hour of rest at room temperature;
- ❖ Divide the dough into two equal parts, form two dough balls and let them rise for about 2 hours;
- ❖ Stretch out the dough as if it were a regular pizza but leaving the low edge;
- ❖ Proceed with cooking; if you don't have an oven that doesn't reach high temperatures, you could use the pan and grill cooking method.
- ❖ Have a look at the tips in chapter 1 regarding home and non-home cooking methods;Spread the hazelnut cream on the hot pizza and add som raspberry, marshmallow and sprinkle some icing sugar.

47) Sicilian Tuna and Basil Pizza Recipe

Preparation Time:

Cooking Time:

Servings:

Ingredients:
- ✓ 1/2 clove garlic minced (crushed)
- ✓ 4 tablespoons chopped canned tomatoes
- ✓ 1 tablespoon tomato paste
- ✓ 1 tsp extra virgin olive oil
- ✓ 1/2 tsp sea salt
- ✓ 1/4 tsp freshly ground black pepper

Directions:
- ❖ Preheat the oven to 230 C/450 F. Mix together the garlic, tomatoes, tomato paste, olive oil, salt and pepper. Spread a thin layer evenly over the pizza crust.

Ingredients:
- ✓ 1 store-bought prebought preinches in diameter)
- ✓ 5 large fresh basil leaves roughly torn
- ✓ 1/2 green pepper (capsicum) finely sliced
- ✓ 6 ounces canned tuna in olive oil drained and broken into small chunks
- ✓ 2 1/2 ounces mozzarella cheese cut into small cubes
- ❖ Arrange the basil, green pepper and tuna evenly over the pizza crust. Place the cubed cheese evenly on top. Place the pizza directly on the oven rack and cook for 12 minutes. Cut into 6 slices to serve.

48) SLOPPY JOE PIZZA

Preparation Time: 30 minutes

Cooking Time: 30 minutes

Servings: 4

Ingredients:
- ✓ 1 pound ground beef
- ✓ 3/4 cup ketchup or sloppy joe sauce
- ✓ 1/2 cup sliced green onions

Directions:
- ❖ Preheat oven to 425F degrees. In large nonstick skillet, brown the ground beef over medium heat 8 to 10 minutes or until no longer pink, stirring occasionally. Drain.
- ❖ Stir in ketchup, green onions and seasoning; heat through.

Ingredients:
- ✓ 1 tsp seasoned salt
- ✓ 1 large prepared pizza crust -12 inch
- ✓ 1 1/2 cup shredded cheese -your choice
- ❖ Place pizza crust on a large baking sheet. Top evenly with beef mixture and sprinkle with cheese. Bake 12 to 15 minutes or until cheese is melted.

49) SLOPPY JOE PIZZA II

Preparation Time: 30 minutes

Cooking Time: 30 minutes

Servings: 4

Ingredients:
- ✓ 1 pound lean ground beef
- ✓ 3/4 cup frozen corn, defrosted
- ✓ 3/4 cup prepared barbecue sauce
- ✓ 1/2 cup sliced green onions

Directions:
- ❖ Heat oven to 425 degrees. In large nonstick skillet, brown ground beef over medium heat 8 to 10 minutes or until no longer pink, stirring occasionally. Pour off drippings.
- ❖ Stir in corn, barbecue sauce, green onions and salt, if desired; heat through.

Ingredients:
- ✓ 1/2 tsp salt (optional)
- ✓ 1 large (16 oz. size) Italian bread shell or prepared pizza crust
- ✓ 1 1/2 cup shredded cheddar cheese
- ❖ Place bread shell on large baking sheet. top evenly with beef mixture; sprinkle with cheese. Bake 12 to 15 minutes or until cheese melts; cut into wedges.

50) SMOKED SALMON AND FENNEL POTATO PIZZA

Preparation Time: 30 minutes   **Cooking Time:** 30 minutes   **Servings: 4**

Ingredients:

- ✓ 2 tablespoons olive oil
- ✓ 1 medium onion
- ✓ 2 cups finely chopped fresh fennel bulb
- ✓ Salt and freshly ground pepper, to taste
- ✓ 1/2 cup white wine
- ✓ 3 medium potatoes, peeled
- ✓ 1/2 cup minced chives or green onion

Directions:

- ❖ Pour oil into a hot frypan, add onions and fennel, saute for 5 minutes. Season with salt and pepper, add wine, lower heat and simmer for 10-15 minutes until vegetables are tender and liquid has evaporated. While fennel is cooking, grate potatoes onto a clean tea towel, roll towel up and sq ueeze grated potatoes dry, transfer to a bowl. Add chives, cornstarch, salt and pepper, toss well to mix.

Ingredients:

- ✓ 1 tbsp cornstarch
- ✓ Salt and freshly ground pepper, to taste
- ✓ 2 tablespoons olive oil
- ✓ 1/2 pound smoked salmon, sliced
- ✓ 2 tbsp minced chives or green onion
- ✓ 3 tbsp sour cream, stirred
- ✓ Freshly ground pepper, to taste

- ❖ Heat a large 10 to 12" (25.530 cm) frypan over medium-high heat, add oil, then the potato mixture. Using a large spatula, press potatoes down to cover bottom of pan evenly, keep pressing down and cook for 5-6 minutes; carefully flip over and continue pressing and cooking for another 5-6 minutes until crusty and golden. Slide onto a platter, spread with the warm fennel, top with smoked salmon and chives, drizzle with sour cream and finish with lots of freshly ground pepper. Serve immediately.

51) SMOKY SALMON PIZZA

Preparation Time: 30 minutes   **Cooking Time:** 30 minutes   **Servings: 4**

Ingredients:

- ✓ 1 can (7-1/2 ozs.) salmon, drained and flaked
- ✓ 1 (12 inch) prepared pizza crust or Italian bread shell
- ✓ cooking spray
- ✓ 1 package (3 ozs.) cream cheese, softened

Directions:

- ❖ Preheat oven to 400 degrees. Place pizza crust on cookie sheet, coat lightly with spray. Spread cream cheese over crust. Add salmon, vegetables, red pepper, and cheese. Bake 10 to 12 minutes until cheese is melted.

Ingredients:

- ✓ 1/2 cup red onion, thin sliced or chopped green onion
- ✓ 1/2 tsp crushed dried red pepper flakes
- ✓ 1 1/2 cup shredded smoked cheese (Swiss, Cheddar or mozzarella)

52) SOUTHWEST BEEF AND CHILE PIZZA

Preparation Time: 30 minutes   **Cooking Time:** 30 minutes   **Servings: 4**

Ingredients:

- ✓   1 pound lean ground beef
- ✓   1/4 tsp salt
- ✓   1 thick prebaked Italian bread shell (12-inch diameter; 16 ounces)
- ✓   1 1/4 cup prepared mild thick and chunky salsa
- ✓   1 1/2 cup shredded Mexican cheese blend or Monterey Jack cheese

Directions:

- ❖   Heat oven to 450 degrees Fahrenheit. In large nonstick skillet, brown ground beef over medium heat 8 to 10 minutes or until beef is no longer pink, breaking up into 3/4-inch crumbles. Season with salt; remove from skillet with slotted spoon.

- ❖   Place bread shell on ungreased pizza pan or large baking sheet. Spread salsa over shell; sprinkle with 1/2 of cheese. Top evenly with beef, chilies, tomatoes, red onion and remaining cheese.

Ingredients:

- ✓   1 can (4 ounces) diced green chilies, drained well
- ✓   2 medium plum tomatoes, seeded, coarsely chopped
- ✓   1/3 cup thin red onion slivers
- ✓   2 tbsp chopped fresh cilantro

- ❖   Bake in 450 degrees Fahrenheit over for 11 to 13 minutes or until topping is hot and cheese is melted. Sprinkle with cilantro; cut into 8 wedges. Serve immediately.
- ❖   serving size: 2 wedges

53) SOUTHWEST BEEF AND CHILE PIZZA

Preparation Time: 30 minutes   **Cooking Time:** 30 minutes   **Servings: 4**

Ingredients:

- ✓   1 pound ground beef
- ✓   1/4 tsp salt
- ✓   1 prepared pizza shell (12 inch size)
- ✓   1 1/4 cup mild chunky salsa
- ✓   1 1/2 cup shredded mexican cheese blend or monterey jack cheese

Directions:

- ❖   Preheat the oven to 450F.
- ❖   In a large nonstick skillet, brown the ground beef over medium heat for 8 to 10 minutes, crumbling it as it cooks. Season with the salt; drain.

Ingredients:

- ✓   4 ounces diced green chilies, drained well
- ✓   2 medium plum tomatoes, seeded and chopped
- ✓   1/2 small red onion, thinly sliced
- ✓   2 tablespoons chopped fresh cilantro

- ❖   Place the pizza shell on an ungreased pizza pan. Spread the salsa over the shell then sprinkle with 3/4 cup cheese. Top with the beef, then the chilies, tomatoes, onion, and the remaining 3/4 cup cheese.
- ❖   Bake for 11 to 12 minutes, or until the topping is hot and the cheese is melted. Remove from the oven and sprinkle evenly with the cilantro. Slice into wedges and serve immediately.

54) SPA PIZZAS

Preparation Time: 30 minutes   **Cooking Time:** 30 minutes   **Servings: 4**

Ingredients:

- ✓ 3 tbsp olive oil
- ✓ 1/2 cup minced onions
- ✓ 1 cup tomato sauce
- ✓ 1/2 tsp oregano
- ✓ 1/4 tsp italian seasoning
- ✓ 3/4 cup sliced mushrooms

Ingredients:

- ✓ 1/2 medium zucchini, thinly sliced
- ✓ 1/2 cup diced red pepper
- ✓ (6• inch) flour or (6-inch) corn tortillas
- ✓ 1/2 cup black olives
- ✓ 1 cup grated mozzarella cheese
- ✓ 1/2 cup diced green pepper

Directions:

- ❖ Heat 2 Tbsp. oil in a heavy medium saucepan over medium heat. Add onions and cook until golden, stirring occasionally, about 5 minutes. Stir in tomato sauce, garlic, oregano and Italian seasoning.
- ❖ Simmer until thickened, about five minutes.
- ❖ Heat remaining 1 Tbsp. oil in skillet over medium deat.

- ❖ Add mushrooms and zucchini and cook until tender, stirring occasionally, about five minutes. Set aside.
- ❖ Preheat oven to 350F. Place tortillas on baking sheet and bake until crisp, about 4 minutes. Spread
- ❖ about 1/4 cup sauce over each. Sprinkle each with 1/4 cup cheese. Top pizzas with mushrooms, zucchini, peppers and olives. Bake until cheese melts, about 5 minutes. Serve.

55) BOBOLI TYPE PIZZA CRUST

Preparation Time: 30 minutes   **Cooking Time:** 30 minutes   **Servings: 4**

Ingredients:

- ✓ 1 cup water
- ✓ 3 cups all purpose flour
- ✓ 1 tsp salt
- ✓ 2 tablespoons olive oil
- ✓ 1 tbsp sugar

Ingredients:

- ✓ 2 tsps Red Star active dry yeast
- ✓ 1 tsp minced garlic
- ✓ 2 tsps parmesan cheese
- ✓ 1/2 tsp Italian seasoning
- ✓ parmesan cheese to sprinkle

Directions:

- ❖ Add all ingredients (except) second parmesan cheese to breadmaker in order listed by your manufacturer. It is a good idea to put the garlic down inside the flour so it does not slow the yeast. Set breadmaker on dough setting.

- ❖ When complete, form two crusts on pizza pans, sprinkle with parmesan cheese, cover and let rise again. Bake 5-10 minutes at about 450 F until light brown. Cool.
- ❖ Wrap tightly in foil and freeze until you get the pizza urge. Great to have around for easy last minute dinners. Good way for kids to make pizza too.

56) CLASSIC PIZZA CRUST

Preparation Time: 30 minutes   **Cooking Time:** 30 minutes   **Servings: 4**

Ingredients:

- ✓ 1 package active dry yeast
- ✓ 2 1/2 cups sifted flour
- ✓ 1 tsp salt

Ingredients:

- ✓ 1 cup warm water
- ✓ 1 tbsp cooking oil

Directions:

- ❖ In a large mixing bowl, combine the yeast, 1 cup of flour, and the salt. Mix. Next, add the water and oil. Beat on low speed for 30 seconds. Scrape the sides of the bowl and continue to beat on high speed for 3 minutes. By hand, stir in enough flour to make the dough stiff. Knead until smooth which can take up to 10 minutes.

- ❖ Place in a well greased bowl and turn the dough until it is lightly greased.
- ❖ Cover and let rise for about 1 1/2 hours or until the dough has doubled in size. Punch it down and chill for 2 hours. Cut the dough in half. On a floured surface, roll the halves into 12 inch circle and about 1/8 inch thick. Brush the surfaces of the dough with olive oil and add the toppings of your choice. Cook at 425for 25 minutes.

57) CORNMEAL PIZZA CRUST

Preparation Time: 30 minutes   **Cooking Time:** 30 minutes   **Servings: 4**

Ingredients:

- ✓ 1 cup warm water
- ✓ 1/4 tsp salt -- optional
- ✓ 2 1/2 cups all-purpose flour -divided
- ✓ 1 cup cornmeal -plus

Ingredients:

- ✓ 1 tbsp cornmeal -- divided
- ✓ 2 tbsp sugar or honey
- ✓ 2 tsp active dry yeast

Directions:

- ❖ Measure carefully, placing all ingredients except 1 tablespoon cornmeal in bread machine pan in order specified by owner's manual. Program basic dough cycle setting; press start. Remove dough from bread machine pan; let rest 2 to 3 minutes.

- ❖ Pat and gently stretch dough into 14-to 15-inch circle. Spray a 14-inch pizza pan with nonstick cooking spray; sprinkle with remaining 1 tbsp cornmeal. Press dough into pan.
- ❖ Follow topping and baking directions for individual recipes. 1 14-inch crust makes 8 servings

58) DEEP DISH PIZZA CRUST

Preparation Time: 30 minutes   **Cooking Time:** 30 minutes   **Servings: 4**

Ingredients:

- ✓ 3 cups all-purpose flour
- ✓ 1/8 cup olive oil
- ✓ 2 jumboeggs -room temperature
- ✓ 2 tablespoons thyme

Directions:

- ❖ Whisk together water, yeast and sugar in a bowl and set aside to proof for 10 minutes. In a large bowl sift together flour and salt and sprinkle in thyme. Mix eggs into yeast mixture. Pour liq uid into dry ingredients and mix until a soft sticky dough forms. remove dough to a lightly floured surface and knead 5 minutes, until dough is no longer sticky.

Ingredients:

- ✓ 1 cup warm water
- ✓ 1 package rapid rise yeast
- ✓ 2 tsp sugar

- ❖ Place in a well oiled bowl, turning to coat all sides, cover and allow to rise until doubled in bulk 2 - 3 hours.
- ❖ Punch dough down and place into a well oiled 12" pizza pan. using your hands, move dough around the bottom of the pan and 2/3 the way up the sides. Set aside and let rise 10 minutes. Brush crust lightly with olive oil and add toppings.

59) EASY PIZZA DOUGH

Preparation Time: 30 minutes   **Cooking Time:** 30 minutes   **Servings: 4**

Ingredients:

- ✓ 3 1/2 cups unbleached, all-purpose flour
- ✓ 2 packages dry active yeast
- ✓ 1 tsp salt
- ✓ 1/2 tsp sugar

Directions:

- ❖ In a mixing bowl fitted with a dough hook, place flour, yeast, salt and sugar. While mixer is running, gradually add water and knead on low speed until dough is firm and smooth, about 10 minutes. Turn machine off. Pour oil down inside of bowl. Turn on low once more for 15 seconds to coat inside of bowl and all surfaces of dough with the oil. Cover bowl with plastic wrap. Let dough rise in warm spot until doubled in bulk, about 2 hours. Preheat oven to 500 degrees F. If using a pizza stone, place stone in oven on bottom rack, preheat oven 1 hour ahead. Punch dough down, cut in half.

Ingredients:

- ✓ 1 1/2 cup lukewarm water from the tap
- ✓ 1/2 tsp olive oil
- ✓ Flour, for the work surface
- ✓ Cornmeal, to dust

- ❖ Place half of the dough on generously floured work surface. By hand, form dough loosely into a ball and stretch into a circle. Using floured rolling pin, roll dough into large circle until very thin. Don't worry if your circle isn't perfect and if you get a hole just pinch the edges back together. To prevent dough from sticking to counter, turn over the dough and sprinkle with flour. Also, flour the counter top and rolling pin as needed. Sprinkle pizza peel or cookie sheet generously with cornmeal. Transfer dough to pizza peel or cookie sheet with no lip. Add toppings. Slide dough onto pizza stone or place cookie sheet with pizza on bottom rack. Bake 10 to 12 minutes or until golden. Roll out remaining dough and top with desired toppings or freeze in freezer bags.

60) HEART SHAPED PIZZA

Preparation Time: 30 minutes   **Cooking Time:** 30 minutes   **Servings: 4**

Ingredients:

- ✓ 1 cup water
- ✓ 2 tablespoons milk
- ✓ 2 tsps sugar
- ✓ 1 1/4 tsp salt
- ✓ 1 tbsp shortening

Directions:

- ❖ Place water, milk, sugar, salt, shortening and olive oil in bowl of food processor and pulse to dissolve sugar and salt.
- ❖ Add yeast,semolina or corn meal, bread flour and all purpose flour. Process until a soft ball forms. Remove from machine and allow to rest, covered with a towel, about 45 minutes.
- ❖ OR to make by hand: Use only all-purpose flour. Place water, milk, sugar, salt, shortening and olive oil in bowl and dissolve sugar and salt.

Ingredients:

- ✓ 1 tablespoon olive oil
- ✓ 1 tablespoon durum semolina (or corn meal)
- ✓ 1 cup unbleached all-purpose flour
- ✓ 2 cups unbleached bread flour
- ✓ 1 1/4 tsp yeast

- ❖ Stir in yeast, semolina or corn meal, all purpose flour and knead to form a soft, but not-too sticky dough (8-10 minutes). Allow to rest, covered with a towel about 45 minutes.
- ❖ Deflate dough very gently before using and allow it to rest 15 minutes more before using in a recipe. You may refrigerate dough in an oiled plastic bag for up to two days.
- ❖ Shape dough into a heart. Top with your favorite sauce and toppings. Bake in a hot oven 425 - 450°F. for 15 - 20 minutes.

61) HERB PIZZA DOUGH

Preparation Time: 30 minutes   **Cooking Time:** 30 minutes   **Servings: 4**

Ingredients:

- ✓ 1 package Active Dry Yeast
- ✓ 1 tsp Sugar
- ✓ 7/8 cup Warm Water -- 110 degrees
- ✓ 1/4 cup Italian Seasoning
- ✓ 2 1/4 cups Flour

Directions:

- ❖ Stir together the yeast,sugar and warm water. Let stand until foamy, about 10 minutes. In the work bowl of a food processor fitted with the steel blade, chop the herbs. Turn off machine.Add flour and salt.
- ❖ Turn themachine on and off a couple of times. While the machine is running, add yeast. Process until the dough forms a ball at the side of the bowl. Add garlic olive oil and process for 30 to 40 seconds more.

Ingredients:

- ✓ 1 tablespoon Flour
- ✓ 1/2 tsp Salt
- ✓ 1 tablespoon Garlic Olive Oil -as needed
- ✓ Oil And Cornmeal For Pan

- ❖ Transfer dough to a bowl that has been oiled with olive oil. Turn the dough until the entire surface has been coated with the oil. Cover bowl with a damp towel and allow to rise in a warm draft free place for 1 hour or until doubled.
- ❖ Roll out on a lightly floured surface and if dough is too elastic, try tossing it from hand to hand to flatten it out. Lightly grease the pizza pan with a little oil and sprinkle with cornmeal. Place the dough on the pizza pan and trim the edges. Bake for 10 minutes 425 F degrees.
- ❖ Remove from oven, lightly brush the crust with a little more oil. Top as desired. Makes enough dough for one 12" crust.

62) PIZZA DOUGH EXCLUSIVE

Preparation Time: 30 minutes   **Cooking Time:** 30 minutes   **Servings: 4**

Ingredients:

- ✓ 1 1/2 tsp bread machine yeast
- ✓ 3 cups all-purpose flour
- ✓ 3/4 cup milk
- ✓ 2 tbsp olive oil

Directions:

- ❖ Place all ingredients except water in a food processor. Pulse to mix well. Then turn machine on and drizzle the water in until it forms a ball. Let the ball go around a few times in the machine to knead it a bit. Remove dough onto a floured surface and knead well for a few minutes until elastic. Place in a greased bowl and let rise until doubled. Remove from bowl and punch down. Cut into 2 pieces and roll out into 4 medium size crusts, enough to feed 4 people.

Ingredients:

- ✓ 1/2 cup lukewarm water
- ✓ 1 1/2 tsp salt
- ✓ pinch sugar

- ❖ Turn oven on and preheat at 400°F for 30 minutes, if using pizza stone. If no stone, preheat oven to 400°F for 10-15 minutes. Place pizza crust on the back of a baking sheet that has been covered with a sprinkling of cornmeal. Place in oven and bake for 8 minutes. Remove and cover with toppings. Place back in oven and bake for 8 more minutes until crust is golden and cheese is bubbly.

63) NEW YORK STYLE PIZZA DOUGH

Preparation Time: 30 minutes   **Cooking Time:** 30 minutes   **Servings: 4**

Ingredients:

- ✓ 1 1/2 cup warm water
- ✓ 2 1/2 tsp granulated sugar
- ✓ 2 1/2 tsps salt
- ✓ 1 tbsp olive oil

Directions:

- ❖ In a large bowl, dissolve sugar and salt in water. Add oil and flour to bowl and stir with heavy spoon for 1 minute. Turn dough out onto a lightly floured surface and press into a circle.
- ❖ Sprinkle yeastevenly over dough and knead for 12 minutes. Divide dough into portions: 4 equal portions for calzones, 3 eq ual portions for 8" pizzas, 2 eq ual portions for 12" pizzas. Place dough balls in a bowl, cover with plastic wrap, and allow to rise for 1 1/2 hours in a warm location. Place a dough ball on a lightly floured surface and sprinkle a light coating of flour on top. Working from the edges to the center, press dough into a circle.

Ingredients:

- ✓ 4 1/2 cups all-purpose flour
- ✓ 1/2 tsp active dry yeast
- ✓ 1/2 cup cornmeal
- ✓ sauce, cheese, and toppings of your choice

- ❖ Preheat a pizza stone in a 500 degree oven for 1 hour. Coat a large cutting board with cornmeal and place the flattened dough onto the cornmeal. Spread sauce over crust and top with cheese and desired toppings. Gently shake the cutting board from side to side, assuring it isn't sticking to the board.
- ❖ For a calzone, fold the crust over in half. Slide the pizza/calzone from the cutting board directly onto the stone in the oven. Bake in 500 degree oven for pizza/calzone from the cutting board directly onto the stone in the oven. Bake in 500 degree oven for 25 minutes, until crust is golden.

64) NEW YORK-STYLE PIZZA CRUST

Preparation Time: 30 minutes   **Cooking Time**: 30 minutes   **Servings: 4**

Ingredients:

- ✓ 2/3 cup warm water
- ✓ 1/2 tsp salt
- ✓ 2 1/4 cups all-purpose flour

Ingredients:

- ✓ 1 tsp sugar
- ✓ 2 tsp active dry yeast
- ✓ 1 tbsp cornmeal -- optional

Directions:

- ❖ Measure carefully, placing all ingredientsexcept cornmeal in bread machine pan in order specified by owner's manual. Program dough cycle setting; press start. Remove dough from bread machine pan; let rest 2 to 3 minutes.
- ❖ Pat and gently stretch dough from edges until dough seems to not stretch anymore. Let rest 2 to 3

- ❖ Let rest 2 to 3 minutes more. Continue patting and stretching until dough is 12 to 14 inches in diameter.
- ❖ Spray 12-inch pizza pan with cooking spray; sprinkle with cornmeal, if desired. Press dough into pan. 3. Preheat oven to 450°F. Follow topping and baking directions for individual recipes, baking pizza on bottom rack of oven.

65) PIZZA CRUST

Preparation Time: 30 minutes   **Cooking Time**: 30 minutes   **Servings: 4**

Ingredients:

- ✓ 0.47 L warm water (110F - 115F)
- ✓ 59 milliliters olive oil
- ✓ 2 packages yeast

Ingredients:

- ✓ 1 2/5 L all-purpose flour
- ✓ 9 9/10 milliliters of salt yellow cornmeal

Directions:

- ❖ Proof yeast with slat in warm water. Mix yeast, water and olive oil, stir in flour 1 cup at a time. Turn out onto floured surface, knead until smooth, 5 to 7 minute, adding flour as necessary. Dough will be soft. Place in oiled bowl, turning to coat all sides, cover with plastic wrap

- ❖ let rise in warm place until doubled. Punch down and let rest 15 mins. Divide in half an, press out into tow 12 inch round pizza pans or 10x15x1 pans or 1 of each. sprinkled with yellow cornmeal(prevents crust from sticking).

66) Pizza Dough (Bread Machine) Recipe

Preparation Time: **Cooking Time**:   **Servings**:

Ingredients:

- ✓ 1 cup water PLUS"PLUS" means this ingredient in addition to the one on the next line, often with divided uses
- ✓ 2 tablespoons water
- ✓ 2 tbsp oil

Ingredients:

- ✓ 2 tbsp oil
- ✓ 3 cups bread flour
- ✓ 1 tsp sugar
- ✓ 1 tsp salt
- ✓ 2 1/2 tsp active dry yeast

Directions:

- ❖ Place ingredients in pan in order listed or as directed per machine instructions. Select white dough cycle. Makes two 12 inch regular crusts or one 16 inch deep dish crust.

- ❖ Top with desired toppings and bake at 400°F for 18-20 minutes or until crust is light brown.

67) PIZZA DOUGH AND SAUCE

Preparation Time: 30 minutes   **Cooking Time**: 30 minutes   **Servings: 4**

Ingredients:

Pizza Dough
- ✓ 3/4 tbsp yeast
- ✓ 1 1/2 cup water
- ✓ 1 1/2 tsp salt
- ✓ 3 tablespoons oil
- ✓ 4 cups flour

Pizza Sauce
- ✓ 6 ounces can tomato paste

Ingredients:

- ✓ 1/2 cup wine or water
- ✓ 1 tsp oregano
- ✓ 1 tsp salt
- ✓ 1 tablespoon sugar
- ✓ 1 tablespoon vegetable oil or olive oil
- ✓ 1 1/2 tablespoon parmesan cheese

Directions:

- ❖ Dissolve yeast in water (You can add a pinch of sugar). Stir in salt, oil and half of flour. Gradually add remaining flour, mixing well. Knead 8-10 minutes or until smooth and elastic. Place in greased bowl and let rise until double (1/2-1 hour). Punch down and let rise again until double.

- ❖ Punch down and divide. Pan out on pizza pans. Top with pizza sauce and toppings.

- ❖ Bake at 400 for Punch down and divide. Pan out on pizza pans. Top with pizza sauce and toppings. Bake at 400 for 25 minutes.

- ❖ Pizza Sauce: Mix all ingredients together, blending well (You can also add a few sprinkles of garlic powder if you want).

- ❖ Top with meats, cheese and other toppings.

68) POLENTA PIZZA CRUST

Preparation Time: 30 minutes   **Cooking Time**: 30 minutes   **Servings: 4**

Ingredients:

- ✓ 1 tbsp Active dry yeast
- ✓ 1 tablespoon Barley malt extract
- ✓ 1 cup warm water
- ✓ 3/4 cup semolina

Ingredients:

- ✓ 1 cup unbleached all purpose flour
- ✓ 3/4 cup polenta/corn meal
- ✓ 1 tsp salt
- ✓ 3 tablespoons extra virgin olive oil

Directions:

- ❖ In a large bowl or electric mixer, dissolve the yeast and barley malt in warm water. Add the semolina, flour, polenta, salt, and olive oil. Combine well. Knead the dough until it is shiny and smooth, adding flour as needed.. Place the dough in a lightly oiled bowl, cover with plastic wrap and let rise until doubled, about 2 hours.

- ❖ When dough has risen, punch down and roll out to a large circle and transfer to a baking sheet or pizza pan. Top with any preferred topping and bake in a preheated 425F oven for 20 -25 minutes. This is good topped with roasted veggies.

69) POURABLE PIZZA CRUST

Preparation Time: 30 minutes   **Cooking Time:** 30 minutes   **Servings: 4**

Ingredients:

- ✓ 3 tablespoons Instant High-Active dry yeast
- ✓ Warm water (110 degrees F)(just enough to dissolve the active yeast)
- ✓ 7 pounds All-purpose or bread flour
- ✓ 1 package (1 lb 2 1/2 oz.) Instant nonfat dry milk

Ingredients:

- ✓ 8 3/4 ounces Sugar
- ✓ 1 1/4 tsp Salt
- ✓ 1/8 cup Olive oil
- ✓ Cornmeal

Directions:

- ❖ Dissolve dry yeast in warm water.=20 Let stand 5 minutes. Place flour, milk, sugar, and salt in mixer bowl. Using a whip, blend on low speed for 8 minutes. Add dissolved yeast and oil. Blend on medium speed for 10 minutes. Batter will be lumpy. Oil three sheet pans (18" x26" x1"). Sprinkle each pan with 1 oz (approximately 3 Tbsp) cornmeal.

- ❖ Pour or spread 3 lb 6 oz (1 1/2 quart) batter into each pan. Let stand for 25 minutes. Bake until crust is set: Conventional Oven: 475 degrees F, 10 minutes. Convection Oven: 425 degrees F, 7 minutes. Top each prebaked crust with desired topping. Bake until heated through and cheese is melted: Conventional Oven: 475 degrees F, 10-15 minutes. Convection Oven: 425 degrees F, 5 minutes.

70) SOFT PIZZA DOUGH

Preparation Time: 30 minutes   **Cooking Time:** 30 minutes   **Servings: 4**

Ingredients:
- ✓ 1 frozen loaf bread dough
- ✓ The best pizza dough I have used is thawed out frozen bread dough. Allow dough to defrost. Roll outto fit pan.
- ✓ Thin Crust Pizza Dough Recipe
- ✓ 3 cups bread flour

Ingredients:
- ✓ 7/8 cup warm water
- ✓ 1 tablespoon vegetable shortening (Crisco)
- ✓ 1 tsp active dry yeast
- ✓ 1 tsp salt
- ✓ 1/2 tsp sugar

Directions:

❖ In a heavy-duty stand mixer fitted with dough hook, add the water, shortening, yeast, and sugar. Mix thoroughly until yeast has fully dissolved. Add flour and salt. Mix on low until most of the flour and water has mixed, then continue kneading for 10 minutes. The dough will be loose and scrappy at first and will eventually form a cohesive ball. There should be no raw flour or crumbs remaining in the bowl.

❖ The dough will be somewhat dry and dense. Place the dough ball into a large bowl and cover tightly with plastic wrap. Let the dough rise for 24 hours in the refrigerator before using. Please note that I cannot over-emphasize the importance of a 24-hour rising time since it is absolutely essential so that the dough will develop its signature texture and, more importantly, its unique flavor! Do not skip this step!

❖ Preheat your oven to 500 F about one hour before you plan to bake the pizza. Turn the dough out onto a large surface and dust with flour. Using a heavy rolling pin, roll the dough out very thin to form a 24-inch or larger circle.

❖ If you're using a cutter pizza pan (recommended), dust the pan lightly with flour, place the dough in the pan and dock. Use the rolling pin to trim off the excess dough drooping over the sides of the pan. If you wish to cook the pizza directly on a pizza stone (not using a pan), then place the dough on a dusted pizza-peel, dock, and fold the edge over 1-inch all the way around and pinch it up to form a raised lip or rim.

❖ Next, precook the crust for 4 minutes before adding any sauce or toppings. Remove the crust from the oven and pop any large air pockets that may have formed.

❖ Add your sauce, shredded mozzarella cheese, and your favorite toppings. Continue baking, rotating the pan half way through so that it cooks evenly, until crust is sufficiently browned and crisp, about 10 to 15 minutes. Remove the pizza from the oven and slide pizza out of cooking pan onto a large wire cooling rack or cutting board. Allow to cool for 5 minutes before transferring to a serving pan. This step allows the crust to stay crisp while it cools, otherwise the trapped steam will soften the crust. Once cool, use a pizza cutter to slice the pie into pieces and enjoy!

71) WHOLE WHEAT PIZZA CRUST

Preparation Time: 30 minutes   **Cooking Time:** 30 minutes   **Servings: 4**

Ingredients:

- ✓ 1 1/4 cup warm water
- ✓ 1/4 tsp salt -optional
- ✓ 2 tablespoons honey or sugar
- ✓ 2 cups all-purpose flour -divided

Ingredients:

- ✓ 1 cup whole wheat flour
- ✓ 2 tsps active dry yeast
- ✓ 1 tablespoon cornmeal

Directions:

❖ Measure carefully, placing all ingredients except cornmeal in bread machine pan in order specified by owner's manual. Program dough cycle setting; press start. Remove dough from bread machine pan; let rest 2 to 3 minutes.

❖ Pat and gently stretch dough into 14pan; let rest 2 to 3 minutes. Pat and gently stretch dough into 14inch circle. Spray 14-inch pizza pan with nonstick cooking spray; sprinkle with cornmeal, if desired. Press dough into pan. Follow topping and baking directions for individual recipes. 1 thick 14-inch crust is 8 servings

72) FIREHOUSE SAUCE

Preparation Time: 30 minutes   **Cooking Time**: 30 minutes   **Servings: 4**

Ingredients:

- ✓ 1 (6 ounce) can tomato paste
- ✓ 3/4 cup warm water (110 degrees F/45 degrees C)
- ✓ 3 tablespoons grated Parmesan cheese
- ✓ 1 tsp minced garlic
- ✓ 1 tbsp Honey or Splenda if you would like low carb
- ✓ 1 tsp anchovy paste (optional)
- ✓ 3/4 tsp onion powder

Directions:

- ❖ In a small bowl, combine tomato paste, water, Parmesan cheese, garlic, Splenda, anchovy paste, onion powder, oregano, marjoram, basil, ground black pepper, cayenne pepper, red pepper flakes and salt;

Ingredients:

- ✓ 1/4 tsp dried oregano
- ✓ 1/4 tsp dried marjoram
- ✓ 1/4 tsp dried basil
- ✓ 1/4 tsp ground black pepper
- ✓ 1/8 tsp cayenne pepper
- ✓ 1/8 tsp dried red pepper flakes
- ✓ Salt to taste
- ❖ Mix together, breaking up any clumps of cheese. Sauce should sit for 30 minutes to blend. spread over pizza dough and prepare pizza as desired.

73) CLASSIC PIZZA SAUCE

Preparation Time: 30 minutes   **Cooking Time:** 30 minutes   **Servings: 4**

Ingredients:

- ✓ 1/2 onion, minced
- ✓ 1 or more cloves garlic, finely minced
- ✓ 2 tbsp olive or vegetable oil (more if needed)
- ✓ 1 can tomato sauce (16 oz.)
- ✓ 1 can tomato paste (6 oz.)

Directions:

- ❖ Mince onion and garlic. Saute in olive oil until onion is clear and tender. Add rest of the ingredients to skillet and simmer for 15-20 minutes.

Ingredients:

- ✓ 2 tsps sugar (optional) it takes out the bitterness of the tomato
- ✓ 1 tsp basil dried
- ✓ 1 tsp oregano dried
- ✓ 1/2 tsp salt
- ❖ Makes enough sauce for 2 pizzas. Also makes a nice sauce for breadsticks and calzones.

74) SPECIAL PIZZA SAUCE RECIPE

Preparation Time: 30 minutes   **Cooking Time:** 30 minutes   **Servings: 4**

Ingredients:

- ✓ 1 can (15 oz.) tomato sauce
- ✓ 1 tbsp oregano
- ✓ 1 tablespoon basil
- ✓ 1 tsp garlic powder

Directions:

- ❖ Combine ingredients in a small saucepan and cook over low heat. Spread on two pizza crusts; top with favorite toppings.

Ingredients:

- ✓ 1/2 tsp onion powder
- ✓ 2 tablespoons brown sugar, if desired
- ✓ 1 tsp salt
- ✓ 1/2 tsp pepper

75) DELICIOUS PIZZA SAUCE RECIPE

Preparation Time: 30 minutes   **Cooking Time:** 30 minutes   **Servings: 4**

Ingredients:

- ✓ 1 large onion
- ✓ 2 cloves garlic
- ✓ 1 tsp tomato puree (tomato paste)

Directions:

- ❖ Chop onion and garlic, microwave for five minutes (omit this step if you don't have a microwave; it isn't essential but it makes the sauce q uicker to cook).
- ❖ Transfer to saucepan, add tomato puree and stir. Add tinned tomatoes. Season, bring to boil, and

Ingredients:

- ✓ 1 can (14 oz size) chopped tomatoes
- ✓ Seasoning

- ❖ Add tinned tomatoes. Season, bring to boil, and simmer for about 15-20 minutes until it has reduced to a jammy consistency. For seasoning,
- ❖ I usesalt, freshly milled black pepper, Worcestershire sauce and some sort of herbs; fresh basil if I have it, or dried Italian seasoning.

76) PIZZA SAUCE II RECIPE

Preparation Time: 30 minutes   **Cooking Time:** 30 minutes   **Servings: 4**

Ingredients:

- ✓ 3 tablespoons olive oil
- ✓ 3 cloves garlic, minced
- ✓ 28 ounces can whole cooked tomatoes

Directions:

- ❖ Warm olive oil with garlic on medium heat. Stir and cook for 2 to 3 minutes.
- ❖ Add drained and seeded tomatoes along with salt, pepper, oregano and basil then stir and cook

Ingredients:

- ✓ 1 tbsp dried oregano
- ✓ 1 tsp dried basil
- ✓ Salt and pepper to taste

- ❖ Add drained and seeded tomatoes along with salt, pepper, oregano and basil then stir and cook for 20 minutes until thick enough to spread over pizza dough.

77) PIZZA SAUCE III RECIPE

Preparation Time: 30 minutes   **Cooking Time:** 30 minutes   **Servings: 4**

Ingredients:

- ✓ 2 cans (6 ounce) tomato paste
- ✓ 2 cloves garlic
- ✓ 3 tablespoons dried parsley flakes
- ✓ 4 tsp dried onion flakes

Directions:

- ❖ Combine tomato paste, garlic, parsley flakes, onion, oregano, basil and water in 2 q uart saucepan.
- ❖ Cook over medium high heat until mixture boils.

Ingredients:

- ✓ 1 tsp dried oregano
- ✓ 1 tsp dried basil
- ✓ 2 cups water

- ❖ Reduce heat to low and simmer 10 minutes. Cool slightly and spread on pizza crust; top as desired and bake.

78) SOUTH BEACH DIET SIMPLE PIZZA SAUCE RECIPE

Preparation Time: 30 minutes   **Cooking Time:** 30 minutes   **Servings: 4**

Ingredients:

- ✓   1 tbsp tomato paste
- ✓   1 cup tomato puree
- ✓   1/8 tsp crushed red pepper flakes

Ingredients:

- ✓   2 tsp dried oregano
- ✓   2 tsps dried basil
- ✓   2 tsps dried thyme

Directions:

- ❖   Combine all in small saucepan and cook over low heat for 15 minutes, or until sauce thickens.

79) WHITE PIZZA SAUCE RECIPE

Preparation Time: 30 minutes   **Cooking Time:** 30 minutes   **Servings: 4**

Ingredients:

- ✓   6 tablespoons butter
- ✓   6 tbsp olive oil
- ✓   2 tablespoons white wine

Ingredients:

- ✓   1 tsp rosemary
- ✓   1 tsp basil
- ✓   2 cloves garlic; minced

Directions:

- ❖   Saute garlic in butter and olive oil. Add all other ingredients and simmer for 15 minutes.

80) White Pizza Sauce Recipe

Preparation Time: **Cooking Time:**   **Servings:**

Ingredients:

- ✓   1/3 cup flour
- ✓   3/4 tsp salt
- ✓   1/8 tsp pepper
- ✓   1/8 tsp paprika

Ingredients:

- ✓   1/8 tsp onion powder
- ✓   2 cups milk
- ✓   1 tbsp butter

Directions:

- ❖   Put first 5 ingredientsin a saucepan. Gradually whisk in milk until no lumps remain. Heat and stir until boiling and thickened.

- ❖   Stir in butter until melted. Spread on pizza crust; top with favorite toppings. Great with grilled chicken strips on top!

81) FRESH PORCINI MUSHROOM PIZZA

Preparation Time: 30 minutes   **Cooking Time:** 15 minutes   **Servings: ONE 10-INCH PIZZA**

Ingredients:

- ✓ 1 pound fresh porcini mushrooms
- ✓ 3 tbsp Essential Garlic Oil ,divided, plus more for finishing
- ✓ Salt
- ✓ 1 portion Spelt Pizza Dough ,Elevated Pizza Dough

Directions:

- ❖ Wipe the porcini free of any dirt that might still be attached with a damp towel and cut into ⅛-inchthick slices. Toss the sliced mushrooms in 1 tbsp of garlic oil and spread out in a single layer on a half sheet, then season with salt. Roast slowly in the window of the wood oven, 7 to 10 minutes. Allow to cool before building the pizza.

- ❖ Following the directions for a fully prepped oven, make sure your fire is at the desired cooking temperature with a roiling flame and a brushed and cleaned oven floor. You are now ready to make a pizza.

- ❖ Stretch out the dough as shown in "How to Shape a Pizza" (here). Lightly dust your pizza peel with flour. Place your stretched dough directly on the peel and proceed to build the pizza.

Ingredients:

- ✓ 4 ounces imported Fontina Val d'Aosta cheese, grated
- ✓ Parmesan cheese
- ✓ Freshly ground black pepper
- ✓ 2 tbsp torn fresh mint leaves

- ❖ Brush the stretched dough with the remaining 2 tbsp garlic oil and distribute the shredded Fontina evenly over the dough, leaving a ½-inch border all the way around the outside. Distribute the roasted mushrooms evenly. Season with a pinch of salt.

- ❖ Slide the pizza into the oven and bake for 3 to 5 minutes, rotating once or twice to ensure even cooking. Remove the pizza to a cutting board, grate Parmesan cheese over the entire pie, and add a few grinds of black pepper. Scatter the torn mint over all. Slice into 6 or 8 wedges. Brush the crust edges with a quick pass of the garlic oil to finish.

82) MUSHROOM PIZZA WITH CREAM AND EGG

Preparation Time: 40 minutes   **Cooking Time:** about 25 minutes   **Servings:**

Ingredients:

- ✓ 1 cup morel mushrooms, sliced, washed, and drained (see A Closer Look)
- ✓ Salt
- ✓ 2 tbsp unsalted butter
- ✓ 1 tsp chopped fresh thyme
- ✓ 3 thick asparagus spears
- ✓ Extra-virgin olive oil
- ✓ 1 extra-large egg

Directions:

- ❖ Preheat a cast iron skillet large enough to hold the sliced morels in a single layer by placing it in a high-heat section of the oven for 5 minutes. Season the morels with a generous pinch of salt and add to the preheated skillet. Cook until all the liquid in the pan has evaporated and the mushrooms begin to sizzle rather than steam, 8 to 10 minutes. Stir in the butter and thyme and return the skillet to the oven for another 3 minutes. Remove and allow to cool until ready to build the pizza.

- ❖ Prepare the asparagus by snapping off the woody stems and discarding. Using a mandoline, carefully slice the raw asparagus lengthwise, creating paper-thin ribbons. Toss the asparagus ribbons in a small bowl with a splash of olive oil and a pinch of salt.

- ❖ Carefully crack the egg into a small bowl. Discard the watery layer that surrounds the white, taking care to keep the yolk intact.

Ingredients:

- ✓ 1 portion Elevated Pizza Dough (here)
- ✓ 2 tbsp Essential Garlic Oil (here), plus more for finishing
- ✓ ¼ cup shredded part-skim mozzarella
- ✓ 2 tbsp heavy cream
- ✓ Parmesan cheese
- ✓ Freshly ground black pepper

- ❖ Following the directions for a fully prepped oven, make sure your fire is at the desired cooking temperature with a roiling flame and a brushed and cleaned oven floor. You are now ready to make a pizza.

- ❖ 5.Stretch out the dough as shown in "How to Shape a Pizza" (here). Lightly dust your pizza peel with flour. Place your stretched dough directly on the peel and proceed to build the pizza.

- ❖ Brush the stretched dough with the garlic oil and spread the shredded cheese evenly over the dough, leaving a ½-inch border all the way around the outside. Arrange the dressed asparagus ribbons over the dough, followed by the cooked morels. Drizzle the assembled pizza with the heavy cream and season the entire pie with a pinch of salt.

- ❖ Slide the pizza into the oven and bake for 2 minutes to set the bottom of the crust. Remove the pie, carefully tip the cracked egg into the center of the pizza, and return it to the oven. Bake until the egg white is opaque but the yolk is still runny, another 2 to 3 minutes.

- ❖ Remove the pizza to a cutting board, grate parmesan cheese over the entire pie, and add a few grinds of black pepper. Slice into 6 or 8 wedges, being careful to cut around the unbroken yolk. Brush the crust edges with a quick pass of the garlic oil to finish. Enjoy the pizza by dunking a slice into the softly cooked egg yolk.

83) STINGING NETTLE AND CHANTERELLE MUSHROOM PIZZA

Preparation Time: 35 minutes   **Cooking Time:** about 20 minutes   **Servings:**

Ingredients:

- ✓ 2 cups stinging nettles, woody stems removed
- ✓ 8 ounces chanterelle mushrooms
- ✓ Salt
- ✓ 3 tbsp Essential Garlic Oil (here), divided, plus more for finishing
- ✓ 1 portion Basic Go-To Easy Pizza Dough (here)

Directions:

❖ Fill a bowl with water large enough to hold the nettles, and soak them for 5 minutes. Agitate the nettles once or twice to loosen any dirt. Using tongs, lift them from the water, leaving the dirt behind, and drain thoroughly in a colander. Set aside until ready to use.

❖ Wipe away any dirt that may still be attached to the chanterelle mushrooms. Slice them into small chunks of roughly the same size and follow the directions for cleaning mushrooms outlined for morels here .

❖ Following the directions for a fully prepped oven, make sure your fire is at the desired cooking temperature with a roiling flame and a brushed and cleaned oven floor.

❖ Preheat a cast iron skillet, large enough to hold the sliced chanterelles in a single layer, by placing it in a high-heat section of the oven for 5 minutes. Season the chanterelles with a generous pinch of salt and add to the preheated skillet. Cook until all the liquid in the pan has evaporated and the mushrooms begin to sizzle rather than steam, 8 to 10 minutes. Remove the pan and add 1 tbsp of garlic oil to the mushrooms, stirring to evenly coat, and cook for another 2 to 3 minutes. Remove from the oven and allow to cool until ready to build the pizza.

Ingredients:

- ✓ ½ cup Simple Tomato Sauce (here)
- ✓ ½ cup shredded part-skim mozzarella
- ✓ 1 tbsp extra-virgin olive oil
- ✓ Aged pecorino romano
- ✓ Freshly ground black pepper

❖ Stretch out the dough as shown in "How to Shape a Pizza" (here). Lightly dust your pizza peel with flour. Place your stretched dough directly on the peel and proceed to build the pizza.

❖ Brush the stretched dough with the remaining 2 tbsp garlic oil and spread the tomato sauce evenly over the dough, leaving a ½-inch border all the way around the outside. Arrange the shredded cheese, distributing evenly. Spread the cooked chanterelles over the cheese. In a small bowl, dress the nettles with 1 tbsp of olive oil and a generous pinch of salt. Toss using kitchen tongs to avoid being stung. Pile the nettles on the pizza in a liberal heap.

❖ Slide the pizza into the oven and bake for 3 to 5 minutes, rotating once or twice to ensure even cooking. Remove the pizza to a cutting board, shave the aged pecorino romano cheese over the entire pie, and add a few grinds of black pepper. Slice into 6 or 8 wedges. Brush the crust edges with a quick pass of the garlic oil to finish.

84) BLACK TRUFFLE AND FONTINA PIZZA

Preparation Time: 25 minutes   **Cooking Time:** 3 to 5 minutes   **Servings:**

Ingredients:

- ✓ 8 ounces Yellow Finn potatoes, cut into ⅛-inch-thick slices
- ✓ Salt
- ✓ Extra-virgin olive oil
- ✓ 1 portion Elevated Pizza Dough (here)
- ✓ 2 tbsp Essential Garlic Oil (here), plus more for finishing

Directions:

- ❖ In a bowl, toss the potato slices with a generous pinch of salt and moisten with a splash each of olive oil and water. Arrange the potatoes in a single layer on a half sheet and roast in a very hot oven until they begin to take on color and soften, 4 to 7 minutes. Allow the potatoes to cool completely, taste, and adjust the seasoning with more salt if needed. Set aside until you're ready to build the pizza.

- ❖ Following the directions for a fully prepped oven, make sure your fire is at the desired cooking temperature with a roiling flame and a brushed and cleaned oven floor. You are now ready to make a pizza.

Ingredients:

- ✓ 1 fresh black truffle
- ✓ 4 ounces Fontina Val d'Aosta cheese, shredded
- ✓ Parmesan cheese
- ✓ Freshly ground black pepper

- ❖ Stretch out the dough as shown in "How to Shape a Pizza" (here). Lightly dust your pizza peel with flour. Place your stretched dough directly on the peel and proceed to build the pizza.

- ❖ Brush the dough with the garlic oil and sprinkle a pinch of salt over the entire pie. Using a truffle slicer or a mandoline or a very sharp knife, slice the truffle as thinly as possible and cover the entire pie with the slices. Top the truffles with the Fontina, and add a few gratings of Parmesan over all.

- ❖ Slide the pizza into the oven and bake for 3 to 5 minutes, rotating once or twice to ensure even cooking. Remove the pizza to a cutting board and add a few grinds of black pepper. Slice into 6 or 8 wedges. Brush the crust edges with a quick pass of the garlic oil to finish.

85) MEXICAN PIZZA

Preparation Time: **Cooking Time:**   **Servings:**

Ingredients:

- ✓ 1 (12" size) prebaked pizza/bread crust
- ✓ 1 can spicy refried beans (16 oz. size)
- ✓ 3/4 cup medium salsa
- ✓ 1/2 cup cheddar cheese -shredded

Directions:

- ❖ Place crust on large baking sheet.
- ❖ In bowl, combine beans and salsa; spread on crust.

Ingredients:

- ✓ 1/2 cup monterey jack cheese -shredded
- ✓ 1/2 cup green onions -- sliced
- ✓ 1 can sliced black olives -drained (2 1/4 oz. size)
- ✓ 1 tsp cilantro -minced
- ❖ Sprinkle on remaining ingredient except cilantro. Bake at 450 degrees F for 10 minutes. Top with cilantro.

86) MEXICAN PIZZA SPECIAL

Preparation Time: 35 minutes   **Cooking Time:** about 20 minutes   **Servings:**

Ingredients:

- ✓ 1/2 pound Lean Ground Beef
- ✓ 1 cup Salsa
- ✓ 2 cups Shredded Cheddar Cheese
- ✓ 1 1/2 tsp Chili Powder

Directions:

- ❖ In a skillet, brown the Lean Ground Beef. Drain off the excess grease and then add the Chili Powder and Cumin.
- ❖ Spread 1/4 cup of the Salsa on each Flour Tortillas and 1/4 of the cooked beef mixture.

Ingredients:

- ✓ 1/2 tsp Cumin (optional)
- ✓ 4 (10 inch size) Flour Tortillas
- ✓ Chopped Green Pepper, Onions, Mushrooms

- ❖ Top with the Shredded Cheddar Cheese and the toppings of your choice.
- ❖ Bake in a pre Bake in a predegree oven for 8 to 10 minutes.

87) MEXICAN SALMON PIZZA

Preparation Time: 35 minutes   **Cooking Time:** about 20 minutes   **Servings:**

Ingredients:

- ✓ Nonstick cooking spray
- ✓ 2 small purchased baked pizza crusts (about 7 inches in diameter)
- ✓ 1/2 cup bottled salsa or picante sauce
- ✓ 1/2 cup coarsely crushed tostadas

Directions:

- ❖ A packaged combination of Cheddar, Colby and Monterey Jack cheeses with Mexican seasonings.

Ingredients:

- ✓ 1/2 cup cooked, flaked salmon
- ✓ 1/4 cup chopped red onion (optional)
- ✓ 1 cup shredded Mexican seasoned cheeseor Monterey Jack cheese

- ❖ Heat oven to 450°F. Spray top surface of each pizza crust with nonstick spray and place on a baking sheet. Spread half of salsa on each crust. Top each crust with crushed tostadas, salmon, onions and cheese. Bake until cheese is bubbly and lightly browned, 8-10 minutes.

88) MEXICAN STUFFED PIZZA

Preparation Time: 35 minutes   **Cooking Time:** about 20 minutes   **Servings:**

Ingredients:

- ✓ 1 can (15 oz.) chili with beans
- ✓ 1 can (4 oz.) diced green chiles
- ✓ 2 packages (8 oz.) refrigerated crescent roll dough
- ✓ 1/2 cup shredded cheddar cheese

Directions:

- ❖ Preheat oven to 350° F.
- ❖ Combine chili and green chiles in medium bowl. Slightly overlap crescent dough triangles around edge of 10-to 12-inchround pizza pan, positioning top half of each triangle so that it is hanging over the edge of the pan.

Ingredients:

- ✓ 2 cups toppings (shredded lettuce, chopped tomato, sliced
- ✓ ripe olives, chopped onions, guacamole, sour cream
- ✓ and shredded cheddar cheese)

- ❖ Spoon chili mixture in center of each crescent roll triangle; bring top half of each triangle over chili and tuck under pointed end. Sprinkle with cheese.
- ❖ Bake for 30 to 35 minutes at 350F or until golden brown. Top immediately with toppings. Serve hot.

89) TACO BELL MEXICAN PIZZA

Preparation Time: 35 minutes   **Cooking Time:** about 20 minutes   **Servings:**

Ingredients:
- ✓ 1/2 pound ground beef
- ✓ 1/2 tsp salt
- ✓ 1/4 tsp dried minced onion
- ✓ 1/4 tsp paprika
- ✓ 1 1/2 tsp chili powder
- ✓ 2 tbsp water
- ✓ 8 small (6-inch diameter) flour tortillas
- ✓ 1 cup Crisco shortening or cooking oil

Ingredients:
- ✓ 1 (16 oz) can refried beans
- ✓ 1/3 cup diced tomato
- ✓ 2/3 cup mild picante salsa
- ✓ 1 cup shredded cheddar cheese
- ✓ 1 cup shredded Monterey Jack cheese
- ✓ 1/4 cup chopped green onions
- ✓ 1/4 cup sliced black olives

Directions:
- ❖ Cook the ground beef over medium heat until brown, then drain off the excess fat from the pan. Add salt, onions, paprika, chili powder and water, then let mixture simmer over medium heat for about 10 minutes. Stir often. Heat oil or Crisco shortening in a frying pan over medium-high heat. If oil begins to smoke, it is too hot. When oil is hot, fry each tortilla for about 30-45 seconds per side and set aside on paper towels. When frying each tortilla, be sure to pop any bubbles that form so that tortilla lays flat in oil.

- ❖ Tortillas should become golden brown. Heat up refried beans in a small pan over the stove or in the microwave. Preheat oven to 400F. When meat and tortillas are done, stack each pizza by first spreading about 1/3 cup refried beans on face of one tortilla. Next spread 1/4 to 1/3 cup of meat, then another tortilla. Coat your pizzas with two tablespoons of salsa on each, then split up the tomatoes and stack them on top. Next divide up the cheese, onions and olives, stacking in that order. Place pizzas in your hot oven for 8-12 minutes or until cheese on top is melted.

90) TEX-MEX PIZZA

Preparation Time: 35 minutes   **Cooking Time:** about 20 minutes   **Servings:**

Ingredients:
- ✓ 1 (12 inch) Thin Crust Dough shell (uncooked)
- ✓ 2 large Tomatoes, diced
- ✓ 1 tablespoon Chopped jalapeno pepper
- ✓ 4 Green onions, chopped
- ✓ 2 Cloves garlic, minced

Ingredients:
- ✓ 2 cups Cheddar cheese, shredded
- ✓ 2 tablespoons Grated parmesan cheese
- ✓ 1 Avocado, chopped
- ✓ 1/2 cup Sour cream
- ✓ 2 tablespoons Chopped Cilantro

Directions:
- ❖ Spoon tomatoes over pizza dough, leaving a 1/2" border. Top with jalapenos, garlic and onion. Sprinkle with cheeses and season with salt and pepper to taste.

- ❖ Bake in 500 degree oven for 10 to 14 min. until bottom of crust is golden brown. Top with avocado, a dollop of sour cream and cilantro. Pass extra sour cream.

91) ARTICHOKE AND RED PEPPER PIZZA

Preparation Time: 35 minutes   **Cooking Time:** about 20 minutes   **Servings:**

Ingredients:
- ✓ 1 Boboli Thin Pizza Shell
- ✓ 1 tbsp olive oil
- ✓ 1 cup julienne cut red bell pepper
- ✓ 1 tsp dried basil
- ✓ 1 tsp dried oregano

Ingredients:
- ✓ 5 garlic cloves, minced
- ✓ 1 can artichoke hearts, drained and chopped (not in oil)
- ✓ 1 jar sliced mushrooms, drained
- ✓ 1 1/2 cup shredded part skim mozzarella cheese
- ✓ Freshly cracked pepper

Directions:
- ❖ Heat oil in a nonstick skillet, simmer ingredientsuntil tender. Place on boboli shell and top with cheese. Bake at directions on Boboli package.

92) ARTICHOKE PEPPER PIZZA

Preparation Time: 35 minutes   **Cooking Time:** about 20 minutes   **Servings:**

Ingredients:
- ✓ 1 medium red bell pepper
- ✓ 1 tsp olive oil
- ✓ 2 cloves garlic, crushed
- ✓ 1/4 cup light mayo
- ✓ 1/8 tsp red pepper

Ingredients:
- ✓ 1/8 tsp black pepper
- ✓ 1 cup artichoke hearts
- ✓ • pound size) cooked pizza crust (like Boboli)
- ✓ 1 cup shredded mozzarella cheese
- ✓ 1/2 cup crumbled feta cheese
- ✓ 1/2 tsp thyme

Directions:
- ❖ Cut the red bell pepper into strips. Saute in the olive oil in a skillet for 3 minutes. Stir in half the garlic. Saute for 1 minute.
- ❖ Process the remaining garlic, mayo, red pepper, black pepper and artichokes in a food processor until the artichokes are finely chopped.
- ❖ Place the pizza crust on a baking sheet. Spread with the artichoke mixture to within 1/2 inch of the edge. Top with the red bell pepper. Sprinkle with the mozzarella cheese, feta cheese and thyme.
- ❖ Bake at 450 degrees F for 14 minutes.

93) AVOCADO 'N EVERYTHING PIZZA

Preparation Time: 35 minutes   **Cooking Time:** about 20 minutes   **Servings:**

Ingredients:

- ✓ 2 cups buttermilk baking mix
- ✓ 1/2 cup hot water
- ✓ 1 can (8 ounces) tomato sauce
- ✓ 1/4 cup chopped green onion
- ✓ 1/2 cup shredded mozzarella cheese
- ✓ 1/2 cup sliced mushrooms

Directions:

- ❖ Heat oven to 425F. Stir together buttermilk mix and water with fork in small bowl. Pat or roll into Heat oven to 425F. Stir together buttermilk mix and water with fork in small bowl. Pat or roll into inch circle on ungreased baking sheet or pizza pan. Mix together tomato sauce and green onion; spread over pizza dough.

Ingredients:

- ✓ 1/3 cup sliced ripe olives
- ✓ 1 small tomato, sliced
- ✓ 2 tablespoons olive oil
- ✓ 1 avocado, seeded, peeled and sliced
- ✓ Fresh basil leaves, optional

- ❖ Top with cheese, mushrooms, olives and tomato slices. Drizzle olive oil over top. Bake 15 to 20 minutes or until edge of crust is golden brown. Remove pizza from oven and arrange avocado slices over top. Garnish with basil leaves and serve.

94) BELL PEPPER, RED ONION, AND GOAT CHEESE PIZZA

Preparation Time: 35 minutes   **Cooking Time:** about 20 minutes   **Servings:**

Ingredients:

- ✓ 1 (ounce size) fully baked thin pizza crust (such as Boboli)
- ✓ 1/4 cup olive oil
- ✓ 3 cloves garlic, minced
- ✓ 3 cups (packed) baby spinach leaves
- ✓ 1 1/2 cup thickly sliced mushrooms
- ✓ 1/2 cup drained roasted red peppers from jar, cut into thin strips

Directions:

- ❖ Preheat oven to 425F.
- ❖ Place pizza crust on large baking sheet. Mix olive oil and minced garlic in small bowl. Using pastry brush, brush 2 tablespoons garlic oil evenly over crust.

Ingredients:

- ✓ 1/2 cup paper-thin red onion slices
- ✓ 8 large fresh basil leaves, cut into thin strips
- ✓ 1 (ounce size) soft fresh goat cheese, coarsely crumbled (or mozzarella, fontina,
- ✓ gorgonzola)

- ❖ Top with spinach leaves, then sprinkle with sliced mushrooms, roasted red peppers, red onion slices, fresh basil, and crumbled goat cheese. Drizzle pizza evenly with remaining garlic oil.
- ❖ Bake pizza until crust is crisp and cheese begins to brown, about 18 minutes. Transfer pizza to board. Cut into wedges and serve warm.

95) BETTER THAN FROZEN FRENCH BREAD PIZZA

Preparation Time: 35 minutes   **Cooking Time:** about 20 minutes   **Servings:**

Ingredients:

- ✓ 1 loaf crusty French bread
- ✓ 2 individual submarinestyle hard rolls, split lengthwise
- ✓ 3/4 cup prepared low fat chunky or garden style spaghetti sauce
- ✓ 1 tsp dried oregano

Ingredients:

- ✓ 1/2 fresh green pepper, sliced thinly
- ✓ 1/2 cup fresh or canned mushrooms, thinly sliced
- ✓ 1/4 cup fatfree Parmesan cheese
- ✓ 1 cup low fat, shredded mozzarella cheese

Directions:

- ❖ Spoon spaghetti sauce over sliced bread or rolls. Top with mushrooms and green peppers.

- ❖ Sprinkle with oregano and cheeses. Bake in preheated over for 12-15 minutes.

96) BLACK AND WHITE PIZZA

Preparation Time: 35 minutes   **Cooking Time:** about 20 minutes   **Servings:**

Ingredients:

- ✓ 1 Loaf frozen bread dough -thawed
- ✓ 3 large onions -- sliced thin
- ✓ 3 tbsp olive oil
- ✓ 1 1/2 tsp dried sweet basil

Ingredients:

- ✓ Dash Seasoned Salt
- ✓ 16 ounces Black Olives -drained & sliced
- ✓ 8 ounces Mozzarella Cheese -- shredded

Directions:

- ❖ Follow package directions for thawing bread dough. In a large skillet heat oil; reduce heat; add onions. Cover and cook, stirring frequently, until onions are just tender. Stir in seasoning and basil. Grease a cookie sheet and set aside. Roll dough into an 11 x 14 rectangle on a lightly floured surface. Carefully lift dough onto cookie sheet.

- ❖ Gently spread onions and cheese over dough leaving an edge. Sprinkle on olives. Let this rest 15 minutes. Heat oven to 425F degrees. Bake 15 minutes or until crust is golden brown.

97) BROCCOLI MUSHROOM PIZZA

Preparation Time: 35 minutes   **Cooking Time:** about 20 minutes   **Servings:**

Ingredients:

- ✓ 1 tablespoon olive oil
- ✓ 2 cups sliced fresh mushrooms
- ✓ 1 medium onion -- chopped
- ✓ 10 ounces frozen chopped broccoli -thawed and drained

Ingredients:

- ✓ 1 cup spaghetti sauce
- ✓ 1 prepared pizza crust
- ✓ 8 ounces shredded mozzarella cheese

Directions:

- ❖ Preheat the oven to 400°F. Grease a pizza pan or baking sheet. Saute the onions and mushrooms in the olive oil in a large skillet until soft. Stir in the broccoli and cook until liquid is evaporated. Stir in spaghetti sauce; remove from heat.

- ❖ Spoon sauce onto prepared pizza crust, leaving about one inch around the perimeter. Top evenly with cheese. Bake for 15 minutes or until cheese is melted and crust is golden.

98) BROCCOLI PIZZA

Preparation Time: 35 minutes   **Cooking Time:** about 20 minutes   **Servings:**

Ingredients:

- ✓ 1 tablespoon olive oil
- ✓ 1 clove garlic, minced
- ✓ (6 inch) Boboli Pizza Crust
- ✓ 1 package (8 oz) shredded mozzarella cheese, divided
- ✓ 1 cup small broccoli flowerets

Ingredients:

- ✓ 1/2 cup thin red onion wedges,
- ✓ 1/2 cup sliced yellow squash
- ✓ 1/2 cup red pepper strips
- ✓ 1 tablespoon dried oregano leaves

Directions:

- ❖ Preheat oven to 450 F.
- ❖ Mix oil and garlic; brush on pizza crust.

- ❖ Top with 1 cup cheese, broccoli, onion, squash, red pepper, remaining 1 cup cheese and oregano.
- ❖ Bake 8-10 minutes or until cheese is melted.

99) BROCCOLI RABE AND CHICK-PEA PITA

Preparation Time: 35 minutes   **Cooking Time:** about 20 minutes   **Servings:**

Ingredients:

- ✓ 2 cloves garlic -sliced thin
- ✓ 1/4 cup extra-virgin olive oil
- ✓ 1(ounce) can chick-peas -rinsed and drained
- ✓ 1/2 cup water

Directions:

- ❖ Preheat oven to 400°F.
- ❖ In a large heavy skillet cook garlic in oil over moderate heat, stirring, until pale golden. Transfer garlic and 1 tablespoon oil to a food processor. Add chick-peas, 1/4 cup water, and salt and pepper to taste and blend mixture until smooth.
- ❖ Heat oil remaining in skillet over moderately high heat until hot but not smoking and cook broccoli rabe, turning it with tongs, until wilted.

Ingredients:

- ✓ 1 large bunch broccoli rabe, chopped, coarse stems discarded
- ✓ 1/2 tsp dried hot red pepper flakes
- ✓ 3 (6-inch) pita breads split in half to form circles
- ✓ 1/2 cup parmesan cheese -freshly grated
- ❖ Add remaining 1/4 cup water and pepper flakes and simmer, covered partially, until broccoli rabe is crisp-tender and almost all liq uid is evaporated, about 2 minutes.
- ❖ Spread inside sides of pita with chick-pea purée and top with broccoli rabe and Parmesan.
- ❖ Arrange pita pizzas on a large baking sheet and bake in middle of oven 10 minutes, or until edges are golden.

100)   CABBAGE PIZZA

Preparation Time: 35 minutes   **Cooking Time:** about 20 minutes   **Servings:**

Ingredients:

- ✓ 1 onion -minced
- ✓ 3 cloves garlic -- minced
- ✓ 2 tablespoons oil
- ✓ 4 cups chopped cabbage

Directions:

- ❖ In a frying pan, saute, the onion and garlic in the oil for 5 minutes, or until soft. Add the cabbage and fennel seeds, stir well, and cover. Cook over mediumLow hear until the cabbage is just wilted. Preheat the oven to 425F.

Ingredients:

- ✓ 1 tbsp fennel seed
- ✓ 1 cup tomato sauce
- ✓ 1/2 cup Parmesan cheese -freshly grated
- ✓ 1 prepared whole wheat pizza crust
- ❖ Place the pizza crust on a greased baking sheet, and top with the tomato sauce, then the cabbage mixture. Sprinkle with the Parmesan cheese. Bake for 15 to 20 minutes,or until the cheese is lightly browned.

101)   CALIFORNIA PIZZA KITCHEN GRILLED EGGPLANT CHEESELESS

Preparation Time: 35 minutes   **Cooking Time:** about 20 minutes   **Servings:**

Ingredients:

- ✓ 3 Tbsp, Olive oil, divided
- ✓ 1/2 tsp Soy sauce
- ✓ 1/4 tsp Cumin
- ✓ 1 pinch Cayenne pepper
- ✓ 4 Japanese eggplants, sliced lengthwise 1/8-in. thick
- ✓ Pizza dough as needed

Directions:

- ❖ Combine 1 Tbsp. olive oil, soy sauce, cumin and cayenne. Lightly coat both sides of eggplant slices with mixture. Discard outside skin-covered slices.
- ❖ Grill eggplant 2 to 3 minutes per side; set aside.
- ❖ Shape pizza dough into 2 9-in. rounds. Brush each with 1 Tbsp. olive oil. Layer with onions then grilled eggplant.

Ingredients:

- ✓ 2/3 cup Red onion, sliced in 1/8-in. rings
- ✓ 2 tbsp Fresh cilantro, chopped
- ✓ 4 cups Fresh spinach, cut in 1/4-in. strips
- ✓ 6 Oil-packed, sun-dried tomatoes, drained, patted dry, julienned
- ✓ Extra-virgin olive oil optional
- ✓ Balsamic vinegar optional
- ❖ Bake at 500F until crusts are golden, about 8 minutes.
- ❖ Slice pizzas, then top with cilantro and spinach. Garnish with sun-dried tomato. Serve with oil and vinegar on side, if desired.

102)   CARAMELIZED ONION AND GORGONZOLA PIZZA

Preparation Time: 35 minutes   **Cooking Time:** about 20 minutes   **Servings:**

Ingredients:

- ✓ 2 tsp butter
- ✓ 1 large Vidalia onion, thinly sliced
- ✓ 1 tsp sugar

Directions:

- ❖ In a large saute pan, melt butter over medium heat. Saute onions in butter until the onions are soft and dark brown, approximately 25 minutes. Stir in sugar, and continue cooking for 1 or 2 more minutes.
- ❖ Preheat oven to 425 degrees F (220 degrees C).

Ingredients:

- ✓ 1 package (10 ounce size) refrigerated pizza dough
- ✓ 6 ounces Gorgonzola cheese, crumbled
- ❖ Grease a pizza pan or cookie sheet, and press out the dough to desired thickness. Spread onions evenly over the dough, and top with crumbled Gorgonzola.
- ❖ Bake for 10 to 12 minutes, or until done.

103) Caramelized Red Onion Pizza

Preparation Time: 35 minutes   **Cooking Time:** about 20 minutes   **Servings:**

Ingredients:

- ✓ 1 tsp olive oil
- ✓ 3 large red onions, thinly sliced
- ✓ 1 tablespoon maple syrup or light brown sugar.
- ✓ 1 tbsp balsamic vinegar.
- ✓ 2 tsps.dried basil .
- ✓ 2 cups. marinara sauce

Directions:

- ❖ In large nonstick saute pan, heat olive oil over medium heat. Saute onions, stirring freq uently, for about 10 minutes, until caramelized to golden brown. Stir in maple syrup, vinegar and dried basil; set aside.
- ❖ Spread marinara sauce over pizza dough, leaving 1/2-in. border. Arrange

Ingredients:

- ✓ Pizza dough, rolled into 18-to 19-in. round as needed
- ✓ 4 cups. Swiss chard or spinach, shredded
- ✓ 1/2 cup fresh basil, slivered
- ✓ 1/2 cup low-fat feta cheese, crumbled
- ✓ 1/2 tsp dried oregano .
- ✓ 1/4 tsp black pepper

- ❖ Swiss chard on top; top with onions. Sprinkle with fresh basil, feta cheese, oregano and pepper.
- ❖ 4Bake for 30 to 35 minutes at 375F until crust is crisp.

104) CARIBBEAN PIZZA

Preparation Time: 35 minutes   **Cooking Time:** about 20 minutes   **Servings:**

Ingredients:

- ✓ 1 pizza crust
- ✓ 8 ounces tomato sauce
- ✓ 30 ounces black beans -rinsed and drained
- ✓ 8 ounces crushed pineapple -drained

Directions:

- ❖ Preheat oven to 425F. Bake crust for 5 minutes. Spread tomato sauce over partially baked crust. Top with the black beans and pineapple. Drizzle the lime juice over the top. Evenly sprinkle the cilantro and mozzarella cheese on top. Return to the oven and bake for 12-14 minutes or until edges of crust are turning golden and cheese is melted in the center.

Ingredients:

- ✓ 4 tsps lime juice
- ✓ 2 tablespoons fresh cilantro -chopped
- ✓ 6 ounces mozzarella cheese -shredded

- ❖ You can make your own crust, use the refrigerated dough, or a pre-made crust like Boboli for this recipe. If using pre-made, you do not need to partially bake it first unless you want a firmer crust.

105)   Cheese Lovers Pizza Squares Recipe

Preparation Time: **Cooking Time**:   **Servings**:

Ingredients:

- ✓   1 can refrigerated pizza dough
- ✓   1 cup Ricotta cheese
- ✓   8 ounces shredded Mozzarella cheese
- ✓   2 ounces pepperoni, diced

Directions:

- ❖   Preheat oven to 400 F.
- ❖   Press pizza dough into a 15 x 10-inch jelly roll pan. Bake for 12 minutes then remove from oven and spread Ricotta cheese over crust. Top with Mozzarella, pepperoni, tomatoes, pepper and oregano.

Ingredients:

- ✓   2 plum tomatoes, thinly sliced
- ✓   1 cup bell pepper, sliced
- ✓   1 tsp oregano
- ✓   2 tablespoons chopped parsley

- ❖   Return to oven and bake for 6 minutes more or until cheese is melted. Sprinkle with parsley, cut into squares and serve.

106)   CHEESY PEPPER AND MUSHROOM PIZZA

Preparation Time: 35 minutes   **Cooking Time**: about 20 minutes   **Servings**:

Ingredients:

- ✓   1 1/2 cup all-purpose flour
- ✓   1 package active dry yeast
- ✓   1/4 tsp salt
- ✓   1/2 tsp sugar
- ✓   1 tsp cooking oil
- ✓   Nonstick spray coating
- ✓   1 tablespoon cornmeal
- ✓   3/4 cup low-fat cottage cheese, drained

Directions:

- ❖   For crust, mix 3/4 cup of the flour, the yeast, sugar, and salt. Add oil and 1/2 cup warm water (120 degree F to 130 degree F). Beat with electric mixer on low speed 30 seconds, scraping bowl. Beat on high speed 3 minutes. Stir in as much remaining flour as you can. Then, knead in enough remaining flour to make a moderately stiff dough that is smooth and elastic (5 minutes total). Shape into a ball. Place in a greased bowl; turn once. Cover; let rise in a warm place until double (about 30 minutes). Punch down. Cover; let rest 10 minutes.

Ingredients:

- ✓   1 egg
- ✓   2 tbsp grated Parmesan cheese
- ✓   1 tsp dried basil, crushed
- ✓   1 clove garlic, minced
- ✓   1/8 tsp pepper
- ✓   1 medium green or red sweet pepper
- ✓   1 cup sliced fresh mushrooms
- ✓   1 cup shredded part-skim mozzarella cheese

- ❖   On a floured surface roll dough into a 14-inch circle. Place on a pizza pan sprayed with nonstick spray coating and sprinkled with the cornmeal. Build up edges slightly. Bake crust in a 425 degree F oven about 10 minutes or until lightly browned.

- ❖   In a blender container combine cottage cheese, egg, Parmesan, basil, garlic, and pepper. Cover; blend until smooth. Spread over hot crust. Cut green pepper into rings. Place atop pizza with mushrooms. Sprinkle with mozzarella. Bake in a 425 degree F oven 10 minutes until hot.

107)   Cheesy Pizza

Preparation Time: 35 minutes   **Cooking Time:** about 20 minutes   **Servings:**

Ingredients:
- ✓ 1 refrigerated Pizza Crust
- ✓ 1 1/3 ounce shredded Fresh Parmesan cheese
- ✓ 1 tbsp dried basil
- ✓ 1 cup shredded provolone cheese

Directions:
- ❖ Heat oven to 425F degrees. Grease 12-inch pizza pan or 13 x 9-inch pan. Unroll dough and place in greased pan; press out with hands forming 1/2 inch rim. Bake at 425F degrees for 7 to 9 minutes or until light golden brown.

Ingredients:
- ✓ 1 cup shredded Cheddar cheese
- ✓ 1 cup shredded Monterey Jack
- ✓ 1 1/4 cup spaghetti sauce

- ❖ Sprinkle partially baked crust with parmesan cheese and basil. Top with provolone, Cheddar and Monterey Jack cheese. Drizzle spaghetti sauce over the cheese. Bake at 425F degrees for 12 to 18 minutes or until crust is deep golden brown.

108)   CHICAGO STYLE SPINACH PIZZA

Preparation Time: 35 minutes   **Cooking Time:** about 20 minutes   **Servings:**

Ingredients:
- ✓ 1 can (10 oz.) refrigerated pizza crust
- ✓ 1 package (10 oz.) chopped spinach, thawed, well drained
- ✓ 1 package (16 oz.) partskim mozzarella cheese, shredded
- ✓ 1/4 cup (1 oz.) Parmesan cheese, shredded, divided

Directions:
- ❖ Heat oven to 500 degrees. Press pizza crust onto bottom and sides of well greased 10 inch deep dish pizza pan or 9 x 13 inch baking dish. Mix spinach, mozzarella cheese and 2 tablespoons Parmesan. Spread evenly over crust.

Ingredients:
- ✓ 1can (28 oz.) tomatoes, drained, cut up
- ✓ 2 garlic cloves, minced
- ✓ 2 tsps dried oregano leaves
- ✓ 1/2 tsp red pepper flakes, optional

- ❖ Mix tomatoes, garlic, oregano and pepper flakes. Spread over cheese mixture. Sprinkle with remaining 2 tablespoons Parmesan cheese. Bake 10 minutes. Reduce heat to 375 degrees and bake for an additional 20 minutes.

109) CLASSIC CHEESE PIZZA

Preparation Time: 35 minutes   **Cooking Time**: about 20 minutes   **Servings**:

Ingredients:

- ✓ 1 ounce fresh yeast or 1/2 ounce dried yeast
- ✓ 1 pinch sugar
- ✓ 1/2 pint lukewarm water
- ✓ 14 ounces plain flour
- ✓ 1 tsp salt (scant)
- ✓

Ingredients:

- ✓ 1/4 pint olive oil
- ✓ 3/4 pint tomato and garlic sauce
- ✓ 1 pound mozzarella, cut into 1/4 inch dice
- ✓ 6 tablespoons Parmesan, freshly grated

Directions:

- ❖ Crumble the fresh yeast or sprinkle the dried yeast and a pinch of sugar into 3 tbsp of lukewarm water. Be sure that the water is lukewarm (110 - 115 F. neither too hot nor too cold to the touch). Let it stand for 2 to 3 minutes, then stir the yeast and sugar into the water until completely dissolved. Put the cup in a warm, draught-free place for 3 to 5 minutes, until the yeast bubbles up and the mixture almost doubles in volume. If the yeast does not bubble, start over again with fresh yeast.

- ❖ Sift the flour and salt into a large, warmed bowl. Make a well in the centre of the flour and pour in the yeast mixture, 3/8 pint of lukewarm water and 3 tbsp of the olive oil. Mix the dough with a fork or your fingers.

- ❖ When you can gather it into a rough ball, place the dough on a floured board and knead it for about 15 minutes, until smooth, shiny and elastic. Dust the dough lightly with flour, put in a large clean bowl and cover. Place the bowl in a warm, draught-free spot for about 1 1/2 hours, until the dough has doubled in bulk.

- ❖ Now preheat the oven to 450 F. Punch the dough down with your fists and break off about one quarter of it to make the first of the 4 pizzas. Knead the small piece on a floured board or a table for a minute or so, working in a little flour if the dough seems sticky. Flatten the ball into a circle about 1 inch thick with the palm of your hand. Hold the circle in your hands and stretch the dough by turning the circle and pulling your hands apart gently at the same time.

- ❖ When the circle is about 7 or 8 inches across, spread it out on the floured board again and pat it smooth, pressing together any tears in the dough. Then roll the dough with a rolling pin, from the centre to the far edge, turning it clockwise after each roll, until you have a circle of pastry about 10 inches across and about 1/8 inch thick.

- ❖ Crimp or flute the edge of the circle with your thumbs until it forms a little rim. Dust a large baking sheet lightly with corn meal and gently place the pizza dough on top of it.

- ❖ Knead, stretch and roll the rest of the dough into 3 more pizzas.

- ❖ Pour 6 tablespoons of the tomato sauce on each pizza and spread it with a pastry brush or the back of a spoon.

- ❖ To make a cheese pizza, sprinkle the sauce with 6 tablespoons of mozzarella and 2 tablespoons of grated parmesan. Dribble 2 tablespoons of olive oil over the pizza and bake it on the lowest shelf or the floor of the oven. Reduce the oven temperature to 400 f after 5 minutes and cook for about 10 minutes in all, until the crust is lightly browned and the filling bubbling hot.

110)   COLD VEGETABLE PIZZA

Preparation Time: 35 minutes   **Cooking Time:** about 20 minutes   **Servings:**

Ingredients:

- ✓ 16 ounces cream cheese -Softened
- ✓ 1 cup mayo
- ✓ 1 Envelope Hidden Valley Ranch Dressing
- ✓ 1 package Refrigerated Crescent Rolls

Directions:

- ❖ Preheat oven to 350F degrees. Press out crescent rolls in a jelly roll pan and bake for 8 to 10 minutes. Mix together the cream cheese, mayonnaise and Hidden Valley Ranch Dressing. Pour on top of cooled crescents.

Ingredients:

- ✓ 1/2 cup chopped celery
- ✓ 1/2 cup chopped cauliflower
- ✓ 1/2 cup black olives

- ❖ Spread the chopped vegetables over pan and top with shredded cheese. Chill several hours or overnight

111)   CORN AND TOMATO PIZZA

Preparation Time: 35 minutes   **Cooking Time:** about 20 minutes   **Servings:**

Ingredients:

- ✓ 1 pizza crust
- ✓ 1 1/2 cup frozen corn -thawed
- ✓ 1 1/2 cup plum tomatoes -seeded and chopped
- ✓ 1/4 cup chopped fresh basil
- ✓ 3 cloves garlic -minced

Directions:

- ❖ Prepare Pizza Crust. Preheat oven to 450°F. Combine corn, tomatoes, basil, garlic, oregano and pepper in medium bowl.

Ingredients:

- ✓ 1 tsp dried oregano leaves
- ✓ 1/2 tsp coarse ground black pepper
- ✓ 2 tablespoons dijon mustard -optional
- ✓ 1 cup shredded mozzarella cheese
- ✓ 2 tablespoons grated parmesan cheese

- ❖ Spread mustard over prepared crust, if desired. Sprinkle crust with mozzarella cheese; top with corn mixture and Parmesan cheese. Bake 18 to 20 minutes or until crust is golden brown and cheese is melted. Cut into wedges.

112)   DOUBLE FILLED MUSHROOM PIZZA

Preparation Time: 35 minutes   **Cooking Time:** about 20 minutes   **Servings:**

Ingredients:

Filling 1
- ✓ 1/2 cup Stuffed Olives -sliced
- ✓ 4 ounces Sliced Canned Mushrooms
Filling 2
- ✓ 5 small Scallions -thinly sliced

Directions:

- ❖ Preheat oven to 350F degrees. Slice bread vertically into 10 slices without cutting completely through the bread. Spoon sauce eq ually into each section. Alternate fillings between slices. Sprinkle cheese over fillings. Loosely wrap pizza in heavy aluminum foil. Bake 30 minutes, or until heated through. Open foil; bake 10 to 15 minutes.

Ingredients:

Pizza
- ✓ 1 Loaf French Bread Loaf -14" long
- ✓ 1 Jar Pizza Sauce
- ✓ 1 cup Mozzarella Cheese -shredded

- ❖ We truly hope that you and your family will enjoy these delicious gourmet pizza recpies for years to come! And as always, we love hearing feedback from our customers, so if you enjoyed this book, please consider taking the time to leave a review! Happy Pizza Making!

113) ROSEMARY FOCACCIA

Preparation Time: 2 hours   **Cooking Time:** 20 to 30 minutes   **Servings:**

Ingredients:

FOR THE SPONGE
- ✓ 1½ cups lukewarm water
- ✓ 2 tbsp plus 2 tsp active dry yeast
- ✓ ½ cup extra-virgin olive oil

FOR THE DOUGH
- ✓ 16 ounces (3½ cups) bread flour

Directions:

- ❖ TO MAKE THE SPONGE
- ❖ 1.Put the warm water in the work bowl of a stand mixer and sprinkle the yeast evenly over the surface. Stir to dissolve. Add the olive oil and mix by hand. Set the work bowl in a warm location. 2.After 20 to 30 minutes, you should notice small bubbles beginning to form on the surface of the sponge and a pleasant "bready-yeasty" smell beginning to arise.
- ❖ TO MAKE THE DOUGH
- ❖ Line a half sheet pan with parchment paper.
- ❖ In a large bowl, combine the bread and semolina flours and the salt.
- ❖ Attach the dough hook to your mixer. Mix the sponge on medium-low speed. Gradually add the flour mixture, a cup at a time, allowing the flours to be absorbed into the wet mixture before adding more. Mix thoroughly for 5 minutes, making sure no dry ingredients remain.
- ❖ Using a spatula, scrape out the dough directly onto the prepared sheet pan and gently spread out the dough. Don't worry if it doesn't fully cover the parchment. Allow the dough to rest, uncovered, in a warm spot for 20 minutes.
- ❖ Using your fingers, spread the dough a bit more evenly into the pan, trying to take the dough all the way to the edges.
- ❖ Allow the dough to rest for another 20 minutes and then repeat until the entire sheet tray is covered evenly with the focaccia dough. Allow to rest a final time until the dough has risen and filled the sheet tray completely, another 20 to 30 minutes.
- ❖ You are now ready to top the focaccia. Dip your fingertips in the olive oil and press them into the dough to make shallow dimples all over the surface. Repeat until the entire sheet pan is pockmarked and oily.
- ❖ Mix the rosemary with the remaining olive oil. Dot the surface with the herbs, pressing them gently into the dough, and drizzle any remaining oil over the focaccia. Scatter the salt flakes evenly over the surface. The focaccia is now ready for the oven.

Ingredients:

- ✓ 9¼ ounces (2 cups) semolina flour
- ✓ 1 tbsp kosher salt
- ✓ ¼ cup extra-virgin olive oil
- ✓ ½ cup fresh rosemary leaves
- ✓ 2 tbsp sea salt flakes

- ❖ TO BAKE THE FOCACCIA
- ❖ In your wood-fired oven, allow a medium-hot fire to burn down so it is no longer flaming. You should have a nice mass of glowing embers and a fully heated oven. If you have a laser thermometer, you are looking for a floor temperature of around 425°F.
- ❖ Insert the sheet tray opposite the fire source and bake until the focaccia is puffed and deep golden. I like to rotate the pan frequently; this allows me to check the progress of the bake and also gauge the fire's intensity. If it's too cool, I add a small piece of wood; too hot and I can cover the dough loosely with a piece of heavy aluminum foil to slow the browning on the surface.
- ❖ Approximately 20 minutes of baking should set the dough but, depending on your fire, it may take another 10 minutes. Remove the pan from the oven and allow it to cool slightly.
- ❖ With a sharp knife, cut around the edges of the dough and release it from the pan in one slab. The parchment paper should still be on the baked focaccia, but if it isn't, don't fret.
- ❖ Slide the dough back onto the warm oven floor for a final bake. This ensures a nice, evenly crispy crust.
- ❖ Transfer to a cooling rack. When cool, invert and peel off the parchment paper. Cut into rectangular "fingers" and serve.

114) SWEET DOUGH FOR HAND PIES

Preparation Time: 30 to 40 minutes   **Cooking Time**:   **Servings**:

Ingredients:
- ✓ 4½ ounces (1 cup) all-purpose flour
- ✓ 4½ ounces (1 cup) 00 flour
- ✓ 1 tsp sugar
- ✓ ¼ tsp kosher salt

Ingredients:
- ✓ ¾ cup (1½ sticks) very cold unsalted butter, cut into 12 equal cubes, divided
- ✓ ½ cup ice water

Directions:

❖ In the bowl of a stand mixer fitted with the paddle attachment, mix the two flours, sugar, and salt just to combine.

❖ Add 8 of the butter cubes and mix on low speed until the butter begins to break down and the mixture has a sandy appearance. Stop the mixer and sort through the unformed dough by hand, using your fingers to pinch together any large chunks of butter that remain. Mix on low for 2 or 4 more turns. Add the remaining 4 butter cubes and again mix on low until the butter is slightly incorporated, about 2 minutes. Stop the mixer and remove the work bowl. Repeat the pinching step and make sure there are no remaining large chunks of butter in the mixture.

❖ Make a well in the center of the shaggy mass. Add the ice water to the well and gently cover the water pool with the surrounding dough crumbs. Let the dough stand for 5 minutes to allow it to absorb some of the water.

❖ Mix the dough by hand, quickly and evenly. Knead the dough only long enough so it forms a moist, slightly sticky ball, being careful not to overwork it.

❖ Divide the dough into two equal portions and wrap each in plastic wrap. Flatten each ball into a smooth disc about ½ inch thick. The dough should have a nice, even marbled appearance, streaked with butter.

❖ Refrigerate the dough until ready to use, at least 2 hours and up to 24 hours.

115) ESSENTIAL GARLIC OIL

Preparation Time: 15 minutes   **Cooking Time**:   **Servings**:

Ingredients:
- ✓ bunch spring garlic (4 or 5 shoots), green tops included, or 8 garlic cloves, peeled •.

Ingredients:
- ✓ 1 cup extra-virgin olive oil

Directions:

❖ If you are using garlic shoots, peel away the outer layer to reveal the pale inner layer. Slice off the root end and discard, then split the garlic shoots in half lengthwise

❖ Line up the split garlic shoots and slice crosswise into crescents 1/16 inch thick. Slice the entire white portion and a good deal of the green tops.

❖ You should have about ½ cup sliced garlic in total. 3.If you are using garlic cloves, cut them in half and then cut out the bitter germ that runs down the center, and discard it. Slice the cloves thinly, then chop very finely.

❖ Transfer the garlic to a small bowl and cover with the oil.

116) SIMPLE TOMATO SAUCE

Preparation Time: 5 minutes

Cooking Time:

Servings: MAKES ABOUT 2 CUPS

Ingredients:
- ✓ 1 (28-ounce) can whole peeled tomatoes
- ✓ ¼ cup extra-virgin olive oil

Ingredients:
- ✓ 3 or 4 fresh basil leaves
- ✓ 2 tsp salt

Directions:
- ❖ This could not be simpler. Open the can of tomatoes and add the oil, basil leaves, and salt. Using the wand of an immersion blender, purée until smooth.

- ❖ Taste and adjust the seasoning with salt or olive oil.
- ❖ Or, transfer the ingredients to a countertop blender or food processor and purée until well incorporated.

117) OVEN-ROASTED RED SAUCE

Preparation Time: 10 minutes

Cooking Time: 20 minutes

Servings:

Ingredients:
- ✓ 2 fresh basil sprigs
- ✓ ½ yellow onion, thinly sliced

Ingredients:
- ✓ 3 pounds ripe organic tomatoes, such as Early Girl or Roma, cored • ¼ to ½ cup extra-virgin olive oil
- ✓ 1 tbsp salt
- ❖ Halfway through, move the dish to the middle of the oven so the tomatoes cook a bit more slowly.
- ❖ Remove the gratin dish and allow it to cool slightly. Transfer the entire contents to a food mill and pass it through. The basil stems, tomato skins, and most of the seeds will be left behind, and you will have a thin purée. If you prefer, return the purée to the gratin dish and reduce further in the oven for a more concentrated sauce.
- ❖ The sauce will keep in an airtight container in the refrigerator for up to 1 week or in the freezer for up to 2 months.

Directions:
- ❖ Line the bottom of the gratin dish with the basil sprigs, followed by the onion slices, and finally the tomatoes, cored-side down. Drizzle the entire dish with the olive oil so the vegetables are well coated, and sprinkle the salt over all.
- ❖ Build a nice hot fire with a generous bed of coals. Place the gratin dish directly next to the active coal bed, as close to the fire as possible, but not in the embers. Select a small piece of wood and add it to the fire to create some extra heat and a bit of smoke as the wood catches.
- ❖ Roast the tomatoes until they are noticeably charred, bubbling, and somewhat collapsed, about 20 minutes.

118)   PIZZA WITH FENNEL SAUSAGE, PEPPERS, AND CALABRIAN CHILES

Preparation Time: 20 minutes   **Cooking Time**: about 10 minutes   **Servings**:

Ingredients:

- ✓   ¾ cup thinly sliced sweet bell peppers
- ✓   1 yellow onion, thinly sliced
- ✓   Extra-virgin olive oil
- ✓   Salt
- ✓   4 ounces fennel sausage, casing removed, crumbled
- ✓   1 portion Basic Go-To Easy Pizza Dough

Directions:

- ❖   Combine the peppers and onion in a small bowl, moisten with enough olive oil to thoroughly coat the vegetables, and season with salt. Set aside to soften slightly for 10 minutes.

- ❖   Following the directions for a fully prepped oven, make sure your fire is at the desired cooking temperature with a roiling flame and a brushed and cleaned oven floor.

- ❖   Place the crumbled fennel sausage in a cast iron skillet and brown in the oven, about 5 minutes. Remove from the pan and drain the fat.

- ❖   Stretch out the dough as shown in "How to Shape a Pizza" (here). Lightly dust your pizza peel with flour. Place your stretched dough directly on the peel and proceed to build the pizza.

- ❖   Brush the stretched dough with the garlic oil and spread the tomato sauce evenly over the dough, leaving a ½-inch border all the way around the outside.

Ingredients:

- ✓   2 tbsp Essential Garlic Oil ,plus more for finishing
- ✓   ¼ cup Simple Tomato Sauce
- ✓   ½ cup shredded part-skim mozzarella
- ✓   1 tbsp Calabrian chile purée (see A Closer Look)
- ✓   2 tbsp flat-leaf Italian parsley

- ❖   Top the pie with the mozzarella cheese. Season the entire pie with a pinch of salt.

- ❖   Lift the peppers and onions from the bowl and allow any excess liquid to drain off. Spread evenly over the pizza. Arrange the crumbled sausage over the pie.

- ❖   7lide the pizza into the oven and bake for 3 to 5 minutes, rotating once or twice to ensure even cooking. Remove the pizza to a cutting board. Slice into 6 or 8 wedges.

- ❖   In a thin drizzle, garnish the cooked pizza with the Calabrian chile purée. Brush the crust edges with a quick pass of garlic oil to finish. Garnish with the parsley leaves.

119) FOUR SEASONS PIZZA

Preparation Time: 30 minutes   **Cooking Time:** about 10 minutes   **Servings:**

Ingredients:

- ✓ ½ cup wild mushrooms such as black trumpets or chanterelles
- ✓ Extra-virgin olive oil
- ✓ Salt
- ✓ 1 portion Basic Go-To Easy Pizza Dough
- ✓ 1 tbsp Essential Garlic Oil ,plus more for finishing
- ✓ ¾ cup Simple Tomato Sauce
- ✓ ¼ cup Basic Pesto
- ✓ ¾ cup shredded part-skim mozzarella

Ingredients:

- ✓ 2 fresh basil leaves
- ✓ 2 whole salt-packed anchovy fillets, rinsed, soaked, filleted (see Prep Tip here), and halved
- ✓ lengthwise (8 pieces total)
- ✓ 2 ounces smoked ham, thinly sliced
- ✓ 1 ounce crumbled Gorgonzola
- ✓ Parmesan cheese
- ✓ Freshly ground black pepper

Directions:

- ❖ Toss the mushrooms with a little olive oil and salt and roast them in a cazuela in the oven until they are wilted and slightly caramelized, about 7 minutes. Set aside to cool.

- ❖ Following the directions for a fully prepped oven, make sure your fire is at the desired cooking temperature with a roiling flame and a brushed and cleaned oven floor. You are now ready to make a pizza.

- ❖ 3.Stretch out the dough as shown in "How to Shape a Pizza" (here). Lightly dust your pizza peel with flour. Place your stretched dough directly on the peel and proceed to build the pizza.

- ❖ Brush the stretched dough with the garlic oil and spread the tomato sauce evenly over three-quarters of the dough, leaving a ½-inch border. Spread the pesto over the last quarter of the dough. Arrange the shredded mozzarella over the entire pie.

- ❖ Garnish the pesto portion with the basil leaves. Garnish another quarter with the anchovy fillets, and another with the cooked wild mushrooms. For the last quarter, lay down the ham slices and dot with the Gorgonzola. You should have four distinct sections.

- ❖ Slide the pizza into the oven and bake for 3 to 5 minutes, rotating once or twice to ensure even cooking. Remove the pizza to a cutting board, grate Parmesan over the entire pie, and add a few grinds of black pepper. Slice into four quarters and those quarters into bite-size pieces for all to enjoy. Brush the crust edges with a quick pass of garlic oil to finish.

120) SALAMI PIZZA WITH PARSLEYPARMESAN SALAD

Preparation Time: 10 minutes   **Cooking Time:** 3 to 5 minutes   **Servings:**

Ingredients:

- ✓ 1 portion Basic Go-To Easy Pizza Dough
- ✓ 3 tbsp Essential Garlic Oil ,plus more for finishing
- ✓ ½ cup Oven-Roasted Red Sauce
- ✓ ½ cup shredded part-skim mozzarella
- ✓ 10 thin slices imported dry salami, preferably Tuscan-style

Ingredients:

- ✓ ½ cup fresh flat-leaf parsley leaves
- ✓ ¼ cup shredded Parmesan cheese
- ✓ Salt
- ✓ Extra-virgin olive oil

Directions:

- ❖ Following the directions for a fully prepped oven, make sure your fire is at the desired cooking temperature with a roiling flame and a brushed and cleaned oven floor. You are now ready to make a pizza.
- ❖ Stretch out the dough as shown in "How to Shape a Pizza" (here). Lightly dust your pizza peel with flour. Place your stretched dough directly on the peel and proceed to build the pizza.
- ❖ Brush the stretched dough with the garlic oil and spread the red sauce over the dough, leaving a ½inch border. Top with the shredded mozzarella and the thinly sliced salami, covering the entire surface of the pie by overlapping the salami rounds.

- ❖ Slide the pizza into the oven and bake for 3 to 5 minutes, rotating once or twice to ensure even cooking. Remove the pizza to a cutting board and cut into 6 to 8 wedges. Brush the crust edges with a quick pass of garlic oil to finish.
- ❖ In a small bowl, toss the parsley and Parmesan together, then dress with a pinch of salt and a few drops of olive oil. Mound the parsley salad in the center of the pizza and encourage guests to get a bit of green with every slice they enjoy.

121)   FENNEL SAUSAGE AND WILTED GREENS PIZZA WITH FRESH MOZZARELLA

Preparation Time: 20 minutes   **Cooking Time:** 25 minutes   **Servings:**

Ingredients:

- ✓ 1 yellow onion, diced
- ✓ 1 bunch Swiss chard, leaves stripped from stems, stems reserved (optional)
- ✓ 2 tbsp extra-virgin olive oil, divided
- ✓ Salt
- ✓ 4 ounces fennel sausage, casing removed, crumbled

Ingredients:

- ✓ 1 portion Whole-Wheat Pizza Dough
- ✓ 2 tbsp Essential Garlic Oil ,plus more for finishing
- ✓ ¼ cup Simple Tomato Sauce
- ✓ 4 ounces buffalo mozzarella, thinly sliced

Directions:

- ❖ Following the directions for a fully prepped oven, make sure your fire is at the desired cooking temperature with a roiling flame and a brushed and cleaned oven floor. You are now ready to make a pizza.

- ❖ Combine the yellow onion dice with the chard stems, if using, in a cast iron skillet, and season with 1 tbsp of olive oil and a pinch of salt. Sauté the vegetables slowly, in the window of the oven, until tender, about 8 minutes. Set aside until ready to use.

- ❖ Repeat with the chard leaves in the same manner, seasoning and sautéing slowly until wilted. Stir often to prevent burning and add a splash of water if the pan dries out. Combine the onion-stem mixture and the cooked chard.

- ❖ Place the crumbled fennel sausage in a cast iron skillet and brown in the oven, about 5 minutes. Remove from the pan and drain the fat.

- ❖ Stretch out the dough as shown in "How to Shape a Pizza" .Lightly dust your pizza peel with flour. Place your stretched dough directly on the peel and proceed to build the pizza.

- ❖ Brush the stretched dough with the garlic oil and spread the tomato sauce evenly over the dough, leaving a ½-inch border all the way around the outside. Top the pie with the vegetable mixture and the sliced mozzarella cheese. Season the entire pie with a pinch of salt. Arrange the crumbled sausage over the greens and cheese.

- ❖ Slide the pizza into the oven and bake for 3 to 5 minutes, rotating once or twice to ensure even cooking. Remove the pizza to a cutting board. Slice into 6 or 8 wedges. Brush the crust edges with a quick pass of garlic oil to finish.

122) WHOLE-WHEAT PIZZA WITH PANCETTA, POTATO, AND ASPARAGUS

Preparation Time: 30 minutes

Cooking Time: about 10 minutes per pizza

Servings:

Ingredients:

- ✓ 8 ounces Yellow Finn potatoes, sliced ⅛ inch thick
- ✓ Salt
- ✓ Extra-virgin olive oil
- ✓ 2 thick asparagus spears
- ✓ 1 portion Whole-Wheat Pizza Dough ,divided into two equal balls
- ✓ 2 tbsp Essential Garlic Oil ,plus more for finishing

Directions:

- ❖ Following the directions for a fully prepped oven, make sure your fire is at the desired cooking temperature with a roiling flame and a brushed and cleaned oven floor.

- ❖ In a bowl, toss the potato slices with a generous pinch of salt and moisten with a splash each of olive oil and water. Arrange the potatoes in a single layer on an unlined half sheet pan and roast in a very hot oven until they begin to take on color and soften, 4 to 7 minutes. Allow the potatoes to cool completely, taste, and adjust the seasoning with more salt if needed. Set aside until you're ready to build the pizza.

- ❖ Prepare the asparagus by snapping off the woody stems and discarding. Using a mandoline, carefully slice the raw asparagus lengthwise, creating paper-thin ribbons. Toss the asparagus ribbons in a small bowl with a splash of oil and a pinch of salt.

Ingredients:

- ✓ ½ cup Salsa Bianca
- ✓ ½ cup shredded Fontina cheese
- ✓ 6 ounces pancetta, thinly sliced
- ✓ Parmesan cheese
- ✓ Freshly ground black pepper

- ❖ Stretch out one piece of dough as shown in "How to Shape a Pizza" (here). Lightly dust your pizza peel with flour. Place your stretched dough directly on the peel and proceed to build the pizza.

- ❖ Brush the stretched dough with the garlic oil and spread half of the salsa bianca over the pizza. Distribute half of the shredded Fontina evenly over the dough, leaving a ½-inch border all the way around the outside. Add half of the cooked potato slices and half of the asparagus to the pie. Season with a pinch of salt. Top with half of the pancetta.

- ❖ Slide the pizza into the oven and bake for 3 to 5 minutes, rotating once or twice to ensure even cooking. Remove the pizza to a cutting board, grate Parmesan cheese over the entire pie, and add a few grinds of black pepper. Slice into 4 wedges. Brush the crust edges with a quick pass of garlic oil to finish.

- ❖ 7.Repeat with the second pizza.

123) APPLEWOOD SMOKED BACON AND SUNNY-SIDE UP EGGS WITH PARMESAN

Preparation Time: 10 minutes   **Cooking Time:** 5 to 7 minutes   **Servings:**

Ingredients:

- ✓ 1 portion Whole-Wheat Pizza Dough
- ✓ 1 tbsp Essential Garlic Oil ,plus more for finishing
- ✓ ½ cup Salsa Bianca
- ✓ ¼ cup shredded part-skim mozzarella
- ✓ ½ cup thinly sliced red onion

Ingredients:

- ✓ 4 ounces uncooked thinly sliced applewood smoked bacon or precooked thicker bacon • 2 eggs
- ✓ Salt
- ✓ Parmesan cheese
- ✓ Freshly ground black pepper

Directions:

- ❖ Following the directions for a fully prepped oven, make sure your fire is at the desired cooking temperature with a roiling flame and a brushed and cleaned oven floor. You are now ready to make a pizza.

- ❖ Stretch out the dough as shown in "How to Shape a Pizza" (here). Lightly dust your pizza peel with flour. Place your stretched dough directly on the peel and proceed to build the pizza.

- ❖ 3.Brush the stretched dough with the garlic oil and spread the salsa bianca over the dough, leaving a ½inch border. Top with the shredded mozzarella and the thinly sliced onion, followed by the uncooked bacon (if using).

- ❖ Slide the pizza into the oven and bake for 2 minutes to set the bottom of the pie. Remove from the oven and crack the eggs carefully onto the pizza. Season the eggs with salt. Return to the oven and cook for 3 to 5 minutes longer, rotating once or twice to ensure even cooking. Remove the pizza to a cutting board when the bacon has cooked through and the egg whites are set but the yolks remain soft.

- ❖ Grate Parmesan cheese over the entire pie and add a few grinds of black pepper. Garnish with the precooked bacon (if using). Brush the crust edges with a quick pass of the garlic oil to finish. Enjoy as a proper breakfast, with a knife and fork.

124)   PIZZA WITH CHORIZO Y PAPAS, FRESH CILANTRO, AND LIME

Preparation Time: 40 minutes   **Cooking Time**: 30 minutes   **Servings:**

Ingredients:

- ✓ 1 russet potato, peeled and cut into ½-inch dice
- ✓ 4 ounces Mexican-style chorizo, crumbled
- ✓ 1 portion Basic Go-To Easy Pizza Dough (here) or Spelt Pizza Dough (here) • 2 ounces Cotija cheese, crumbled

Ingredients:

- ✓ 2 tbsp crème fraîche
- ✓ ¼ cup chopped fresh cilantro leaves and stems
- ✓ 1 lime

Directions:

- ❖ Cook the potato in boiling salted water until tender, about 10 minutes. Drain well and reserve.
- ❖ Preheat a cast iron skillet for 5 minutes in the wood oven, add the chorizo, and cook in a mediumhot environment for 3 minutes to render some of the fat. Add the cooked potato to the skillet, stir to combine, and return to the oven. Continue to cook until the chorizo is cooked through and the potatoes receive some color, about 3 minutes more. Remove and set aside to cool completely.
- ❖ Following the directions for a fully prepped oven, make sure your fire is at the desired cooking temperature with a roiling flame and a brushed and cleaned oven floor. You are now ready to make a pizza.

- ❖ Stretch out the dough as shown in "How to Shape a Pizza" (here). Lightly dust your pizza peel with flour. Place your stretched dough directly on the peel and proceed to build the pizza.
- ❖ Spread the chorizo and potato mixture over the stretched pizza crust in a thin, even layer, leaving a ½-inch border around the pizza. Top with the crumbled Cotija cheese.
- ❖ Slide the pizza into the oven and bake for 3 to 5 minutes, rotating once or twice to ensure even cooking. Remove the pizza to a cutting board, drizzle the crème fraîche over the pie, garnish with the fresh cilantro, and squeeze a bit of lime juice over it all. Slice into 6 or 8 wedges.

125)   PIZZA WITH LAMB SAUSAGE, CARAMELIZED ONIONS, AND MARJORAM

Preparation Time: 35 minutes   **Cooking Time:** 30 minutes   **Servings:**

Ingredients:

- ✓   2 yellow onions, thinly sliced
- ✓   2 tbsp extra-virgin olive oil • Salt
- ✓   4 ounces lamb sausage
- ✓   1 portion Elevated Pizza Dough (here)
- ✓   1 tbsp Essential Garlic Oil (here), plus more for finishing

Directions:

- ❖   Following the directions for a fully prepped oven, make sure your fire is at the desired cooking temperature, with a roiling flame and a brushed and cleaned oven floor.

- ❖   Toss the onion slices with the olive oil and salt in a cazuela and roast slowly in the mouth of the oven, tossing frequently. Prevent the onions from burning by adding a splash of water if needed. The onions will lose considerable volume, begin to color slightly, and become much sweeter. When the onions have deeply colored and lost most of their volume, after 20 minutes or so, remove the pan. Allow to cool.

- ❖   Meanwhile, remove the sausage from its casing and crumble into a cast iron skillet. Roast in the oven until the fat begins to render and the meat colors slightly, 3 to 4 minutes. Remove from the skillet, drain the fat, and set aside.

Ingredients:

- ✓   ½ cup Charred Sweet Pepper and Tomato Sauce (here)
- ✓   ½ cup shredded part-skim mozzarella
- ✓   Freshly ground black pepper
- ✓   2 tbsp roughly chopped fresh marjoram

- ❖   Stretch out the dough as shown in "How to Shape a Pizza" (here). Lightly dust your pizza peel with flour. Place your stretched dough directly on the peel and proceed to build the pizza. 5.Brush the stretched dough with the garlic oil and spread the pepper and tomato sauce evenly over the dough, leaving a ½-inch border all the way around the outside. Arrange the shredded cheese on top, distributing evenly.

- ❖   Spread the caramelized onions over the cheese, crumble over the partially cooked lamb sausage, then season the entire pie with a pinch of salt.

- ❖   Slide the pizza into the oven and bake for 3 to 5 minutes, rotating once or twice to ensure even cooking. Remove the pizza to a cutting board and add a few grinds of black pepper. Garnish with the chopped marjoram. Slice into 6 or 8 wedges. Brush the crust edges with a quick pass of the garlic oil to finish.

126) ALSATIAN-STYLE TART OF STEWED ONIONS, BACON LARDONS, AND BLACK PEPPER

Preparation Time: 40 minutes   **Cooking Time:** 25 minutes   **Servings:**

Ingredients:

- ✓ 4 medium yellow onions, thinly sliced
- ✓ Extra-virgin olive oil
- ✓ 1 tbsp salt
- ✓ ¼ cup Alsatian white wine or German-style pilsner beer (optional)
- ✓ 2 portions Basic Go-To Easy Pizza Dough (here)
- ✓ 8 ounces Gruyère cheese, shredded

Ingredients:

- ✓ 1 pound smoked bacon, cut into 1-inch lardons, rendered until slightly crispy, and drained on a paper
- ✓ towel
- ✓ ¼ cup crème fraîche
- ✓ 1 cup fromage blanc cheese
- ✓ Freshly ground black pepper

Directions:

- ❖ Toss the onions with enough olive oil to moisten and season with the salt. Transfer to a cazuela large enough to hold the onions in a single layer and slowly roast in the window of the wood oven for about 15 minutes, stirring often. The idea is to soften the onions but avoid coloring them too much. Add wine, beer, or water if the edges begin to brown too quickly, or if the cazuela dries out. When sufficiently softened, remove from the oven and allow to cool.

- ❖ Brush a half sheet pan with a small amount of olive oil and stretch the dough as outlined in the recipe for Rosemary Focaccia (here). Gradually press the dough into the corners of the pan, eventually filling in the entire rectangle. Allow the dough to rest a few minutes if you are having trouble stretching it and filling in the form.

- ❖ Top the dough with the onions, followed by the Gruyère. Arrange the bacon lardons and press them lightly into the onion mixture. Drizzle the tart with the crème fraîche and finally top with small spoonfuls of the fromage blanc.

- ❖ In a medium-hot oven, bake the tart, rotating often until the dough sets, the onions begin to color, and the bacon crisps. Check to see that the crust is browning nicely by lifting the dough with a spatula. If the tart seems to be cooking too quickly, move the pan to the window where it can cook more slowly and steadily. The total cooking time should be under 10 minutes.

- ❖ If you desire a firm, crisp crust, carefully slide the dough from the pan and finish directly on the hearth floor until crisped and browned.

- ❖ Remove from the oven, transfer to a cutting board, and cut into equal squares. Finish with a generous grinding of black pepper.

127) FENNEL PIZZA WITH BRESAOLA AND LEMON

Preparation Time: 10 minutes   **Cooking Time:** 3 to 5 minutes   **Servings:**

Ingredients:
- ✓ 1 portion Elevated Pizza Dough (here)
- ✓ ½ cup Wild Fennel Sauce (here)
- ✓ 1 cup very thinly sliced fennel bulb, divided
- ✓ Salt

Directions:
- ❖ Following the directions for a fully prepped oven, make sure your fire is at the desired cooking temperature with a roiling flame and a brushed and cleaned oven floor. You are now ready to make a pizza.
- ❖ Stretch out the dough as shown in "How to Shape a Pizza" (here). Lightly dust your pizza peel with flour. Place your stretched dough directly on the peel and proceed to build the pizza. 3.Spread the fennel sauce generously over the dough, leaving a ½-inch border.

Ingredients:
- ✓ 10 thin slices bresaola
- ✓ Juice of ½ lemon
- ✓ Parmesan cheese
- ✓ Freshly ground black pepper

- ❖ In a small bowl, toss half of the sliced fennel with a generous pinch of salt and spread evenly over the dough.
- ❖ Slide the pizza into the oven and bake for 3 to 5 minutes, rotating once or twice to ensure even cooking. Remove the pizza to a cutting board and garnish with the bresaola slices. Slice into 6 or 8 wedges.
- ❖ Dress the remaining fennel slices with the lemon juice and salt, and heap on the pizza. Grate Parmesan over the entire pie and add a few grinds of black pepper.

AUTHOR BIBLIOGRAPHY

THE PIZZA COOKBOOK:

100+ Innovative Recipes for Crusts, Sauces, and Toppings for Every Pizza Lover! How to Make Perfect Focaccia, whether Classic, Meat & Cheese and Much More!

THE HOMEMADE PIZZA:

Learn How to Make the Real Italian Pizza like a Restaurant, using Fresh and Natural Food Ingredients, and Special Pizza and Focaccia Dough! 90+ Italian Style Recipes to Try!

EASY PIZZA RECIPE BOOK:

80+ Authentic Italian Pizza Recipes. A Complete Cookbook: to Learn Special Pizza and Focaccia Dough for Homemade Pizza from scratch! Many Gourmets Toppings Suggestion for Every Taste!

ORIGINAL ITALIAN PANINI COOKBOOK:

More Than 80+ Perfect-Every-Time Recipes for Making Italian Panini - and Lots of Ideas to Make Classical Sandwich Tastier!

QUICK & EASY SANDWHICH

Step-By-Step Recipes to Make Delicious Simple Panini Fast to Prepare at Home Complete Guide Cookbook with 80+ Recipes Easy to Prepare!

GOURMET PANINI COOKBOOK

A Complete Guide to Making Gourmet Tasty and Original Panini for Any Occasion with 80 + Recipes: Simple Step-By-Step Guide to Making Delicious, Tasty and Easy Panini to Create!

DIY PIZZA

2 Books in 1: The Italian Pizza: Special Favorite Pizzas, From Thin Crust to Deep Dish! 150+ Recipes to Make the Real Italian Pizza like a Restaurant, using Fresh and Natural Food Ingredients, and Special Pizza and Focaccia Dough!

THE NATURAL FOOD PIZZA

2 Books in 1: The Pizza Made Using Natural Ingredients for a Healthy Eating with Friends and Family! 150+ Recipes to Try! Choose to Cook Tasty and Healthy!

THE HAMBURGER AND PANINI COOKBOOK

2 Books in 1: 150+ Delicious Burger and Panini Recipes That Are Juicy and Simple to Make! The Hybrid Italian and American Cuisine for a New Cooking Style!

THE BEST PANINI RECIPES

2 Books in 1: 150+ Recipes of the Best Gourmet Panini Collection to Prepare Quick and Easy Meals with Meat, Fish, and Vegetables! Vegan and Vegetarian Panini are Included!

PANINI SPECIAL RECIPES

2 Books in 1: Easy and Quick Meals Cookbook: 150+ Simple and Delicious Lunch, Snack, and Dinner Recipes! The Original and Only Italian Panini Style in Your Kitchen to Make Special Sandwiches!!

THE MASTER RESTAURANT PIZZA COOKBOOK

3 Books in 1: 250+ New Restaurant Style Pizza Recipes to Became a Special Pizza Maker Chef! Share with Your Friends the Original Italian Pizza and Focaccia!

THE ULTIMATE ITALIAN STYLE RECIPE BOOK

3 Books in 1: 250+ Recipes to Make Original Pizza, Focaccia, and Panini with many Toppings, Sauce, and Ingredients! All Based on Natural Ingredients to Get the Tastiest Flavors and Delicious Meals! Vegan and Vegetarian Recipes Included!

PIZZA AND PANINI FOR FAMILY PICKNICK

3 Books in 1: 250+ New Recipes Ideas to Cook Pizza, Panini, Focaccia, and Sweet Pizza! Many Delicious Easy and Fast to Prepare Meals without Renouncing to Taste!

THE GOURMET SANDWHICH AND PIZZA COOKBOOK

3 Books in 1: 250+ New Recipes Ideas with a Complete Guide to Make Gourmet Tasty and Original Panini and Pizza Occasion! Simple Step-By-Step Guide to Making Delicious, Tasty, and Easy Panini and Pizza to Create!

PIZZA AND PANINI LIKE AN ITALIAN CHEF

4 Books in 1: 350+ Recipes to Prepare Pizza and Focaccia Napoli and Genovese Famous Italian Dough, Sauces, Toppings, and Much More! All Based on Natural Ingredients to Get the Tastiest Flavors and Delicious Meals! Vegan and Vegetarian Recipes Included!

CONCLUSIONS

Now you know the essential parts of any homemade Italian pizza, how to make them, and how to assemble your gustatory masterpiece.

But since knowledge is only half the battle, the things you've learned in this book are only, well, half the pizza. To make it complete, you'll have to try them out. Start by making the dough, one of the sauce recipes, and 3 toppings. And if your first experiment doesn't turn out as you expected, write down what you think didn't work and try again in a different way. Try and try again until you have made a cake.

I sincerely hope the book has succeeded in its mission to stop relying on commercial pizzas and make them at home with easy-to-follow instructions.

CPSIA information can be obtained
at www.ICGtesting.com
Printed in the USA
BVHW012334260621
610447BV00011B/1662

9 781803 002071